A CONSUMER'S GUIDE TO

HOPE

A CONSUMER'S GUIDE TO

HOPE

Where to find it & How to keep it

by
Ruth
O'Lill

A.R.E. Press • Virginia Beach • Virginia

A.R.E. Press
Sixty-Eighth & Atlantic Avenue
P.O. Box 656
Virginia Beach, VA 23451-0656

Library of Congress Cataloging-in-Publication Data
O'Lill, Ruth, 1948-
    A consumer's guide to hope : where to find it and how to keep
it / Ruth O'Lill.
        p. cm.
    ISBN 0-87604-313-9
    1. Hope—Religious aspects.   2. Association for Research and
Enlightenment.   I. Title.
BP605.A77O55 1993
291.5—dc20   93-37966

For permission to reprint copyrighted material, grateful acknowledg-
ment is made to: *The Western Journal of Medicine* for excerpts from "The
Medical Uses of Hope," by William Buchholz, M.D. (January 1988, volume 148, page 69), and the University of California at Berkeley *Wellness
Letter* for excerpts from "Where There Is Hope, There Is Life" (May,
1992), © Health Letter Associates, 1992. The Edgar Cayce psychic readings are identified by reading numbers. The original readings are
housed at A.R.E. headquarters in Virginia Beach, Virginia.
    © 1971 Edgar Cayce Readings by the Edgar Cayce Foundation.
                    Reprinted by permission.

Cover design by James Pikaart

Dedication

This book is dedicated to my father, Dr. William Vernon Olcott. He is a philosopher, a fisherman, and a sports fan. A man of great wisdom and delicate humor, he is an open-hearted reservoir of hope.

Table
of Contents

Acknowledgments

I would like to give thanks to the original staff of *Venture Inward* magazine, who took me into its family many years ago. To editor A. Robert Smith, who gave me my start by inviting me to write and then graciously nurturing my style. To Joseph W. Dunn, Jr., then managing editor, who challenged me to write and fight through my doubts, and to Claire Grant, then secretary, who never wavered in her encouragement or her expectations of my ability. Also to Susan Lendvay, now managing editor, who polished my paragraphs before the public saw them.

I also want to thank Dr. Mark Thurston who recommended me for this book project and who kept the concept alive until the time was right to pass it on to me. A special thanks to Cathy Merchand who, as the first person to see the whole project unfold, offered me support. Finally, I want to thank my editor, Jon Robertson, for his patience, his precise and generous editorial direction, and for his ripe sense of humor.

My deepest thanks goes to my best friend, Cheryl Leban, who teased me, praised me, listened to me, and loved me through the whole process. Please know that I thank you all for being such a vital part of this book.

INTRODUCTION

Something about our times cries out for hope. There are nearly countless images and impressions that assault us daily with the message of decline and despair. Our souls are hungry for the nourishment provided by that elusive human experience called hope.

This book powerfully addresses that profound need. No single publication, event, or deed can be the whole answer, but this book is an important contribution to the very ingredient most needed by the human family today: hope.

What exactly is hope? For some of us, what comes to mind most readily is St. Paul's brief list of the most important human virtues: "Faith, hope, love, abide these three" (I Corinthians 13:13). Hope makes it into the top three; but

Paul quickly adds that love is number one. In fact, a lot more has been said and written about love and faith than about hope. Somewhere over the centuries we've lost touch with just how significant and meaningful hope can be to the human condition.

Sad to say, we often use the word in an off-handed, almost superficial way. "I hope the rain ends by tomorrow." Or "You'd better hope to do better in the stock market next year." With comments like these, we reduce hope to little more than a self-centered wish or an idle desire.

But at its essence, hope is something far more. It connects us personally to something bigger about life than we typically perceive. It links us directly to a potent sense of meaning. Hope expands our horizons. It allows our vitality, talents, and good will to resurface.

Yet there is always something a little mysterious about hope. Its source and its mode of operation are never quite explicable. Hope is a step beyond mere confidence. When you're confident, you can point to precise causes for that optimism. In other words, there's usually a clear cause-and-effect rationale for you to feel confident. In contrast, hope often comes when we least expect it or when it seems almost to defy common sense and logical expectation. Hope connects us to the mysterious and hidden forces that make life a real adventure.

Reading this book is sure to give you more hope about your own life and the times in which we live. Some of the stories will remind you of your own hope-enhancing experiences from the past. Other stories will give you a novel perspective on how hope can lift the human spirit.

I'm pleased to have been a small part of the process that has led to this valuable publication. That sequence of events began with an invitation to many thousands of people to explore together this timely subject. The group was the membership of the nonprofit research and educational organization, the Association for Research and Enlightenment, Inc. (A.R.E.). It was founded in the early 1930s by the famous American clairvoyant and spiritual philosopher Edgar Cayce. The membership of this organization seemed like an appropriate group for two reasons. First, the founder had repeatedly stated that the organization's activities should always be based on the principles of helpfulness and hopefulness. In other words, members know that being receptive and responsive to hopeful experiences is right at the heart of the organization's purposes.

Their method was a second reason for conducting such an informal research study on hope with this particular group. Members of the A.R.E. tend to be eagerly engaged in seeking a direct relationship with the hidden, mysterious side of life. For some it means a fascination with psychic phenomena, but for many more it means a genuine search to discover how spiritual forces regularly intersect with material life. Dream study, prayer, and meditation are all ingredients of their spirituality. Although no formula was expected to cause hope, there was reason to believe that sincere, spiritual seekers might well be open and receptive to such experiences.

A call was put forth to these members in the spring of 1991. Each received a description of what Edgar Cayce himself had said about hope and its necessity. Then a simple request was made: help us create a data pool of individual experiences of hope and its impact in their lives. Examples and hints were provided to help participants recall an experience that could be added to this research collection:

• Some people are touched by hope through personal revelation which comes in dreams or meditation.

• Some people experience hope through an intuitive new understanding of what's happening in their lives—a way of knowing that isn't limited by materiality or three-dimensional logic.

• Still other people have experienced hope as a powerful new feeling for the positive potentials of life—less a cognitive way of knowing and more an emotional way of feeling.

The response from the A.R.E. membership was impressive, both in the number of accounts submitted and the inspirational quality of those stories. A total of 382 reports were received.

Clearly there was a story to be told from those narratives. What was needed next was a skillful writer who would identify the patterns and recurrent themes in this extensive information pool. The author of this book, Ruth O'Lill, energetically and joyfully took up that task. The fruits of her careful study and comparisons are presented in *A Consumer's Guide to Hope*.

What impresses me most about her work is the success she had in finding specific qualities embedded within the broader experience that we label "hope." In this work, she has identified sixteen features of hope—ranging from brave to humble, from humorous to exhilarating. (In order to protect the respondents' identities, their names and places of residence have been changed.)

The significance of her analysis shouldn't be missed. By helping us see the individual characteristics of hope—the very qualities and experiences that hope offers to us—we're able to "get a handle" on its meaning. Such a breakdown is a powerful tool, particularly as we deal with the most crucial aspects of human development such as free will, love, and faith. Roberto Assagioli has done this for human volition in his landmark book *The Act of Will*. Other books of this sort include Erich Fromm's *The Art of Loving* and James Fowler's *Stages of Faith*. Although *A Consumer's Guide to Hope* takes a more light-hearted approach than many books of this type, its contribution has a similar effect. In this case it makes the meaning of hope more accessible to us. By understanding its nuances and facets—especially as illustrated by these fascinating real-life stories—it makes hope a little more within our reach. In these times, what could possibly be more important?

Mark Thurston, Ph.D.
Manager of Education
The Association for Research
and Enlightenment, Inc.

1
HOPE
IS AT OUR FINGERTIPS

"Hope is the best possession."
William Hazlitt, *Characteristics*, 1823

I am no stranger to hope and its powers. On many occasions in my life, hope has been an honored member of my family. My most dramatic experience with hope came shortly after my second son was born. His name is Chester. He was born with a red face, a patch of red hair, and a handful of handicaps that included brain damage, a blockage at the base of his stomach, and what would become a permanent hearing loss. Within minutes of his birth, the doctors warned me that he would probably die, then they took him away for a marathon of tests. At first I was devastated and frightened beyond belief. I remember that my face felt as if it were full of needles and the skin under my hair felt as though it were on fire.

1

Twelve hours slowly ticked by before I could see my new son for the second time. Like the rest of the new mothers, I shuffled down the hall, slippers never leaving the floor. I scuffed past the normal pink babies to the special room for special babies and sad-faced mothers. I saw the card that had Chester's name written on it and the huge chart with numbers scratched in blood-red ink. Beneath it struggled my helpless newborn. He was enclosed in a glass womb like a specimen from another planet. The room was filled with the gurgling, beeping, and hissing of machines, and the soft sobbing of new mothers. The infants were silent.

Masked people bent over my baby measuring, monitoring, justifying. I had to squeeze into the only space around him. Someone noticed me and stood erect. The rest of the medical crew exchanged glances, quickly finished what they were doing, and quietly disappeared. I pulled a chair next to my son's square, clear nest and began rocking myself to the rhythm of the life-giving machines that surrounded us.

I couldn't touch him; I couldn't smell him; I couldn't help him. But I could talk to him. I talked to my new son about his big brother waiting at home to meet him. I talked to him about his new room, his yard, his friends waiting to meet him. I talked to Chester about all the wonderful things we were going to do once we got home. I watched him struggle and could do nothing but admire his determination.

My hormones were screaming. I had just spent almost a year getting ready to hold this little person and all I could do was talk to him. And so, I told him softly through the glass, "As long as you're going to try this hard, little man, I promise you, so will I." A voice interrupted us. It was the same bland voice that reminds you to fasten your seat belt in your car. "You'll have to leave now, Mrs. O'Lill," it said. "We've got to do some more tests on him."

My body felt like a bag full of wet towels. I eased out of my chair and moved slowly back past the bright, healthy babies, past the new mothers sitting up in their beds writing out birth announcements. I thought to myself, "What can I announce? The doctors don't even know what is wrong."

Thankfully, my roommate had gone home. All her flowers and nighties and nappies and buttons and bows had gone with her. Her remade bed looked like a flat white board. I collapsed in my rumpled bed, put my empty arms around my pillow, and began to cry—no great sobs or moans, no choking gasps, just a series of whimpers.

In my grief, I never questioned what was wrong with him. I merely prayed that my baby wouldn't die. I knew death well. When I was still a young girl, I had watched my mother die a slow, throbbing death from cancer. I had already spent too many years as a motherless child; I just couldn't become a childless mother. "No, God, not death. I don't need that lesson, I've already learned that one . . . please," I silently cried. "Just let him live."

It may have been hours or maybe only moments later when my hollow shell of motherhood began to fill slowly with warmth. From within, I could feel a mysterious bubbling up of strength and support. Although I was very much alone in my despair, I somehow felt comforted and convinced that I was going to survive this ordeal. One way or another, I was going to get through this incredible fear.

I would not consciously feel that same power surging through me again for many years, but on that day—when I needed the strength to come back into the world and make the best of what I had—the emotional muscles of hope were there for me. I didn't recognize what had happened—this flood of hope filling my shell. Maybe I had expected to see lightning or hear thunder or at least feel awe. Maybe I was just too tired. Instead, I felt only that I was going to live through this.

Chester didn't grow up like other children do, but the doctors were wrong. He lived. Chester is twenty years old now. He's tall, lean, humorous, loving, and healthy. There have been countless times when he was close to death; other times when he was just in danger from the stairs, the streets, or from chunks of meat not small enough to swallow. Even now, each time his well-being is threatened, my heart thunders and my throat closes with fear. But what keeps me sane, what keeps me trying, and what keeps me brave is that feeling of hope that has been forcing back my fears for two decades.

Hope comes in as many forms as Chester's stumbling, choking, stuttering, muffling, blurring disabilities. But hope always comes—to match wits with his challenges, to soften his falls, and to dry his mother's tears. We all need hope. We are truly a planet in need of hope. Life in general has become more complicated, more accelerated, more extended, yet less safe. Given the complexities and challenges of our world, we often forget that we have a proven defense against despair, disease, disillusionment, and even the disinterest we may feel about the world around us. Our best tool for positive survival is hope, and this is a book about what hope is, where to find it, and how to keep it.

In the spring of 1991, Dr. Mark Thurston, manager of education at the Association for Research and Enlightenment (A.R.E.) in Virginia Beach, Virginia, conducted a research project on the nature of hope. He sent questionnaires to the Association members, asking them to recount a personal experience of hope. Within a matter of months, nearly 400 replies came pouring into his office, each describing an inspiring story of how the experience of hope dramatically changed the respondent's life and, in several cases like my own, gave him or her the will to go on.

With such a fruitful response to the research project, Dr. Thurston approached me about the possibility of collecting these stories and turning the project into a book. After we discussed the idea, he handed me an enormous box full of neatly piled reports and I took them home to read. The more I read, the more excited I became about the information. I felt as if I had been given a mountain of oysters and had been invited to find the pearls and string them together into a necklace. I said *yes.*

The commonality of the members' stories is their knowledge of the words and works of Edgar Cayce, the deeply religious clairvoyant who had a unique access to information about the past, present, and future. Although Cayce died in 1945, his life's work is preserved at the A.R.E. where it is still studied by spiritual seekers from all over the world.

Edgar Cayce, known as the "sleeping prophet," is the world's most well-documented psychic. He had the ability to put himself into a trance and respond with amazing insight to questions about the lives and health of the people who came to him for help. The answers that were given to these questions during the sessions are called "readings." The readings not only proved valuable to the people who came to him, but today the information contained in them continues to provide solutions for people from every walk of life. There are over 14,000 recorded discourses, covering a variety of topics, including health, philosophy, and religion, many of which concern the power of hope.

This book is not about a theological definition of hope. It's about how people define hope—hundreds of people who each experienced hope in a sublimely universal way and are about the business of living their own definitions of hope on a daily basis. Each research project participant conveyed his or her own understanding of hope in the report submitted. Some patterns arose from the responses. For the most part, the respondents discussed in this book weren't expecting or even inviting hope into their lives, and they certainly weren't considering whether or not it is a virtue. Instead, they described hope as the reason why they were able to survive a traumatic event, a disease, or the death of someone dear. They also described it as the means by which they were able to move beyond their own overwhelming fear.

According to the personal accounts, hope was experienced through some external trigger or boost that awakened their own internal powers of hope. They describe those moments just before this trigger and then the tangible awareness of hope that emerged. Finally, they explain how the presence of hope in their lives felt. For the participants and myself, hope proved to be our first step back to happiness and, in most cases, to healing our lives.

In nearly every case hope evolved into a trusted tool in the respondent's life. The research revealed that hope has a pattern that can be recognized and is a resource that can be tapped and used endlessly. It has qualities and traits that, on a closer look, can be categorized and called upon at a moment's notice. For the people who answered the questionnaire, hope is more than a virtue; it is an intrinsic power we all possess, a power we can utilize and trust.

Hope arrived in every story; yet it arrived differently in each case. Each visit was custom-made for the person and incident in need of attention. You will see from these fascinating and honest experiences that, at the time, the individuals were not focused on hope. They were too deeply absorbed in their own trauma, depression, despair, or concern. Though many prayed for help, they all related that the help came in the form of hope awakening in them. Hope was the catalyst that reaffirmed their faith. Hope was the process by which they achieved their goal.

For purposes of this research, it is important to note the difference between hope and faith. Though many people generally interchange the two words, several of these accounts describe an experiential distinction between them. For those people who included faith in their recounting (about thirty percent)—they all felt the hopeful experience first and believe that that hopefulness is what helped them through. Subsequently, they now have the faith that hope is at their fingertips. For them, faith is like the foundation or trunk of a tree, while hope is the leaves. The experiences of these particular participants are about how the leaves have reminded them that the faithful tree trunks are warehouses of hope. We all know that there are potential leaves growing on almost every tree, of that we are sure; we have faith in that regard. Now thirty percent of the respondents know that the leaves of hope are cyclical, just like their own personal challenges, and they have faith that the leaves will burst out of the barren branches when the time is right.

As I became more and more absorbed with the stories, I began to look at hope in a different way. To me it became like a prism—a single piece of glass that transforms light into a rainbow of colors. Like a prism, hope reveals a multitude of brightly colored attitudes or shades of experiences. I began to organize all the hopeful experiences according to the many-colored rays that break through the prism of hope. Each vivid ray of hope is explored in its own chapter in this book. For example, "Hope Is Brave," "Hope Is Calm," "Hope Is Strong," and "Hope Is Vast."

It's not surprising that some stories expressed more than one shade or color of hope. In those cases, I chose the brightest hue in order to determine its placement in the book. Take the story of the man who is facing an eighteen-year jail sentence. Though he may need to rely upon many different shades of hope in the future, right now he needs the kind of hope that can make him brave. His story is one example which is included in the "Hope Is Brave" chapter.

Also included in that chapter is the story of a man named John, who confronted a police officer trying to solicit a bribe from him. John's first and only thought was that he would never pay that bribe. John wasn't thinking of hope, he was thinking only of justice. Yet, it was the brave side of hope that emerged from within him and gave him the courage to plant his feet firmly on the ground and refuse the bribe.

A different kind of story came from a woman named Grace, who, just prior to the birth of her second child, discovered that her husband was in love with and indeed leaving her for another man. For her, hope was surprising. No one was more astonished than Grace that her husband had chosen an alternative life style, yet no one could have expected that her frightening and seemingly hopeless situation would lead her to a better marriage, a better career, and a much more rewarding life. Her story, along with other surprises, is in the "Hope Is Surprising" chapter.

The stories also show how hope is humorous, contagious, and determined. In the majority of the stories, project participants were not seeking a certain kind of hope, yet as the stories unfold, it becomes clear that the kind of hope that emerged was exactly suited for each dilemma or need.

Edgar Cayce understood the power of hope. His psychic readings are full of references to being helpful and hopeful in the lives of others as a way to induce our own internal hope. In a reading given for a young man in 1938, Cayce suggested that he try to "bring hope and happiness and joy into the experiences of others." (1643-1) That is certainly a solution worth attempting today. In another reading for yet another person facing a difficult hurdle, Cayce advised, "As ye grow, then, in the grace and mercy of thine own understanding, let this be magnified in the manner and way ye give to others that *expectancy*, that *hope*." (262-121)

The human condition is accompanied by a myriad of challenges that seem to repeat themselves from generation to generation. Another example of Cayce's timely and timeless understanding of the power of hope is from reading 3578-1. Though meant for only one troubled soul many years ago, the message still applies to all of us, for today and for tomorrow. He said, "And that loneliness, that disappointment which has so oft been thine will disappear, and you will come again to those visions of hope, of having a hope. It must first be created in thine own mind, and then there will come into thy experience again the hopes such that with that companionship there may be brought material, mental and spiritual fulfillment..."

The nearly 400 participants in the A.R.E. research project understood the power of hope. Their responses confirmed, over and over again, the many different ways in which hope consistently enabled them to change forever and even to save their own lives. For the respondents, hope is not some entity out there somewhere; it is inside. It is more than a virtue. It is a natural internal resource that needs to be tapped and refined. It's like a muscle that has to be used or it will atrophy. It's as invisible to us as our lungs, our hearts, and our kidneys, but just as vital to our existence.

The majority of respondents described how hope was ignited through an external means—through nature, through a vision, from a dream, an angel, a bird, a deer, a friend, a smile, a letter, or a song. These signs of hope acted as reminders that hope is alive and well and living inside us all. We can selectively choose to incorporate these signs into our lives, no matter what our age, sex, personal philosophy, or belief system.

We all exist with a certain amount of hope on a daily basis. We just don't think much about it. Without this basic element of hope, we wouldn't even get up every morning, let alone perform our daily tasks—a classic symptom of clinical depression. Depression is the direct result of losing our hope. It seems, however, that when we are challenged by disproportionate fear, disorder, disease, and trauma in our lives, that's when we notice a greater need for hope. No one is ever truly hopeless, yet occasionally our "hope tank" gets dangerously low. At that point we need to look for external reminders that will revive our dwindling supply. It's a matter of supply and demand. When our own supply of hope is low, we must be demanding about recognizing the external signs of hope in order to jump-start our recovery.

Hope takes effort. Though it often seems to appear from out of nowhere, hope is really our own private, internal power that sometimes needs to be energized by external circumstances and pulled up from our unconscious to our conscious thoughts. Hope needs to be nurtured, mended, groomed, and honored within us. There are many efficient and predictable ways to achieve a balance in our individual hope "supply-and-demand" formula, a process to fanning the flames of our hope.

You can decide that no matter how horrible a situation may be in your life, you will find something good each day—even if it's a simple word or gesture. You can decide to give a flower or just a smile to a stranger. You can remind yourself that all situations, good or challenging, contain lessons and that, in the bigger picture, they have a purpose. No experience is a waste of time.

You can take steps to work with hope instead of just hoping things will work out. Like several people represented in the research, you can learn to laugh at yourself. You can learn to look for the irony of your situation and chuckle at the circumstances, giving yourself a respite from the pain. Another important lesson is to learn to get out of your own way. Instead of trying to control the dilemma you are in, simply give in and make room for hope.

Letting go worked for Martha from Saginaw, Michigan, who was recently widowed and desperately alone. Upon returning from a visit to the home of her mother, Martha discovered that a water pipe had burst and leaked all over her house. After she went through several hours of tears and self-pity, a neighbor stopped by to help out. As Martha sat on the floor listening to his instructions on how to fill out the insurance forms, she suddenly felt an incredible calm hope surrounding her. She let go of her expectations of herself and allowed hope to enter the empty space. Her story is told in Chapter Three.

There are several ways to invite hope out into the open—into your conscious thoughts. You can, as Cayce suggested, live with hopefulness every day instead of waiting until you are so deep in depression that you have forgotten how to hope. You can practice feeling hopeful every day to ward off illness and keep yourself in balance. The good news is that on those rare occasions when blind-sided by your own pain or shocked by a trauma, hope will still work its way to the surface.

Researchers and health care professionals are beginning to recognize the power of hope. Norman Cousins, in his book *Head First, the Biology of Hope,* wrote about the vital connection between the hopeful attitudes of patients and their rates of recovery. He cited countless cases of seriously ill people who responded favorably to a positive approach toward their own illnesses. Many either recovered or are in remission but, for the ones who didn't survive, their hopeful attitude offered great dignity to their final days on this plane and, for their loved ones, eased the pain of their departure.

A stunning example of the importance of hope in the success of healing comes from *The Western Journal of Medicine* in an article by William M. Buchholz, M.D., entitled "The Medical Uses of Hope" (January 1988, volume 148, page 69). He writes, "As I was eating breakfast one morning I overheard two oncologists discussing the papers they were to present that day at the national meeting of the American Society of Clinical Oncology. One was complaining bitterly: 'You know, Bob, I just don't understand it. We used the same drugs, the same dosage, the same schedule, and the same entire criteria. Yet I got a twenty-two percent response rate and you got a seventy-four percent. How do you do it?'

"His colleague answered, 'We're both using Etoposide, Platinol, Oncovin, and hyperdroxyurea. You call yours EPOH. I tell my patients I'm giving them HOPE. Sure I tell them this is experimental, and we go over the list of side effects together. But I emphasize that we have a chance. As dismal as the statistics are for non-small cell, there are always a few percent who do really well.'"

The academic arena is also beginning to look at hope in terms of its practical potential. Dr. C. Rick Snyder, professor of psychology at the University of Kansas, believes that there is an underlying exactness to the process of hope. In an article in the University of California at Berkeley *Wellness Letter* (May 1992) entitled "Where There Is Hope, There Is Life," Dr. Snyder describes hope as "more than—indeed quite different from—a vague feeling of optimism."

After researching over 4,000 college students on the subject of hope, Dr. Snyder concludes that "hope is a pragmatic, goal-oriented attitude, a stance a person assumes in the face of difficulty." He believes that hopefulness can be taught to anyone and should especially be taught to children. "They should be taught that hope is rarely ever lost and that it can be found and nurtured."

By combining the medical and academic interests in hope with the valuable research from the A.R.E.- sponsored project, we can begin to think of hope as not just a vague afterthought, but rather an attainable and powerful tool with which to embrace the future. We can learn how to find and nurture our hope and, with practice, we can make it a habit.

Such is the beauty of hope. Hope, with all its colors, is flowing inside us like a loving fluid that we often can neither see nor feel—we simply need to trust that it is there. In many of the cases about which you will read, hope emerges in spite of the respondents' lack of effort to be hopeful. Yet, the stories prove that once we experience true hope, know its power, and trust its beauty, we become a part of the process of hope from that day forward. With practice, we can learn to look for hope in each new experience and each new moment ahead of us. For example, a sudden career change doesn't have to mean fear and discomfort. It can mean exciting new challenges and a way to create some new skills. It can be a perfect opportunity to enjoy the many colors of hope.

We've all got some rethinking to do where hope is concerned. Most of us today still might think of hope as merely an elusive feeling that randomly enters and leaves us. We might still misunderstand hope as being something we're either waiting for or missing when it disappears. We may feel impotent against what we perceive to be the whims of hope. While this may seem the case, the reality is that we can orchestrate hope in our lives any time we wish. We can work at feeling hopeful again. We can search for symbols of hope. We can invite our friends to be hopeful with us, and we can trust that hope will happen.

We can learn much from these stories. First, that we are not alone in our darkest times. The hundreds of respondents tell us, in their own words, about fears just like ours and many describe even darker moments than we have known. We can begin to consciously look for the same signs of hope that others have experienced. Hope was reborn for them in a variety of ways, through a simple song on the radio, through dreams and visions, through earthquakes and sunsets, through contact with God. We can learn to reach inside ourselves for the hope that is at our fingertips and call upon its many different dimensions. Finally, as hope begins to happen to us, we can come to our own conclusions. We can write our own definition of hope.

These stories, so graciously contributed by the project participants, are a collection of evidence that, when taken together, proclaim the existence and character of hope. Their experiences are indeed pearls of wisdom from the lives of down-to-earth, everyday people. These pearls, when strung together in a book like this (as I have been honored to do), create a helpful, healing chain to wear every moment as we celebrate our lives.

This collection of personal stories will serve to remind us that we can always bring and keep hope in our lives. No matter how hope comes, it is available to each and every one of us—it is at our fingertips.

2
HOPE
IS BRAVE

"Hope is the survival ring
thrown by the Creator to continue
our journey in the face of all obstacles."

Judy Goring of Monroe, Washington

Hope comes in different sizes, styles, and quantities. Occasionally we find ourselves in a situation that calls for an extra burst of valor or a dose of heroics. Since most of us don't need these qualities on a daily basis, this extra gumption has to be summoned. Fortunately, just beneath the surface, waiting to be called upon like an intrepid warrior standing at attention, is the brave side of hope.

* * *

Jonathan easily remembers his first experience with brave hope. It was the year he bought a brand-new 1949

British A-40 Austin. It was also the year he broke his back. His burst of hope, however, put those two major experiences of that year into the background of his recollections.

He was driving his beautiful new car from St. Louis, Missouri, to Rapid City, South Dakota, with his wife, Cheryl, and his stepdaughter, Mandy. Even though he was in a body cast from his armpits to his buttocks, he did all the driving. He wore a loose shirt and a pair of sweat pants over his plaster of Paris truss. On their way home to Rapid City, at about 2 o'clock in the morning, they were stopped by a policeman outside a small town in Nebraska. It was apparently a police shakedown. The policeman had followed Jonathan and his family well out of town, motioned them off the road, and then parked a distance behind the new Austin.

Jonathan got out of his car and walked back to where the lawman was parked—far away from the ears and eyes of his family. The policeman's door was open and the officer had just swung his body around and pushed his feet to the ground. He was tall even before he stood up. The officer's controlled voice said, "Where are you from?" Jonathan answered, "Rapid City." The policeman nodded from under his hat and then told Jonathan that he had broken their "basic" law. Imagine Jonathan standing there thinking, "I have a broken back and I'm being accused of breaking *their* 'basic' law!"

Jonathan asked what the "basic" law was and all the officer would do was to repeat that he had broken their "basic" law. The policeman finally explained that the best way to solve this problem would be for Jonathan to give him $10 and then he could go on his way. At that point, Jonathan recalls that he became filled with righteous indignation and said to himself with great force and feeling, "I refuse to be a party to this kind of conspiracy!"

For no apparent reason, he became steadfast in his resolve, and somehow he felt protected from almost certain jeopardy. He sensed hope quickly touching every cell in his body. Jonathan knew that he could neither fight nor run in his condition, yet it was obvious to both of them that he would never give that cop a bribe. They met each other's eyes in a silent standoff. Then the cop took a deliberate breath, slowly shook his head, and said, "You don't know how this hurts me."

Despite his pain and fragile situation, Jonathan says he somehow knew it was his moment of truth. He would do what he felt was called for and silently hope it was the right decision. He quickly grabbed the officer's left wrist and shoved his hand against the plaster-cast armor and said, "Hurts you! How the hell do you think I feel?" Shocked, the officer slowly pawed Jonathan's cast and asked, "What is that?" Jonathan answered, "A body cast. I have a broken back." The policeman took another deeper breath to regroup. He asked, "What kind of mileage do you get?" Jonathan said, "Forty on the road." The officer said, "Have a nice trip" and walked away. Jonathan, shaking from his own bravery, quietly said, "Thank you!"

In retelling his story, Jonathan feels that in that one brief moment, hope had rendered him free of the conspiracy and free to go. He believes that at the instant he had decided not to pay that bribe, brave hope had agreed with him. Jonathan trusted his own commitment, and hope emerged with reenforcements to prove to him that he had used his free will wisely.

※ ※ ※

Hal's story of brave hope is a little different from Jonathan's. Jonathan's hope surfaced only for a moment because that was all he needed, but Hal needed an extended supply of hope to outdare the disaster he had created.

Hal considers himself a pretty regular guy, almost average in fact. He says he's always had a very optimistic attitude toward life. He's raised three wonderful children, owned a successful business, and cites those accomplishments as proof of his faith in life. Of course, there were the difficult times that came up (including a divorce and remarriage), but, says Hal, "I dealt with them accordingly and the outcome was always acceptable." Who could have known that hope would be taking up residence at the federal correctional facility that Hal now calls home.

The trouble started in 1984 when he closed his business and soon found himself surrounded by an economic recession. Unfortunately, he was also surrounded by some unsavory people with what he calls "very low vibrations." They offered Hal the opportunity to make a lot of money, and he thought it was a way to pull himself out of the rut he was in. Unfortunately, the authorities also took an interest in Hal's opportunity, which was to illegally manufacture methamphetamine (also known as speed). Within two years he was on his way to federal prison. He quickly pleaded guilty to the charges. Then he was told that, under a new law, the penalty for this crime was 188 months with no parole.

After two years of prison life, Hal finally invited a permanent roommate into his tiny, dingy cell. He called upon hope and explains, "Having just passed my mid-century mark and looking forward to the next one-and-one-half decades of being incarcerated, I decided that it is about time to get my act back together again." He was ready to look inward.

Every warrior needs a shield for his journey and the internal journey can be perhaps the most perilous, but Hal had his artillery. Metaphysics had always been one of his interests, but he never seemed to have enough time to get involved and really study it. Bravely turning the situation around through a new sense of hopefulness, Hal suddenly realized that in prison time was now plentiful. Books on spirituality suddenly became available, and he began to reclaim his self-image and positive outlook.

First, Hal discovered the book *There Is a River*, the biography of Edgar Cayce by Thomas Sugrue, in the prison library. After reading that book, the circumstances of his life began to make some sense to him. He then started to practice yoga and meditation. The tools for spiritual awakening had arrived, and since that time Hal has not stopped re-creating himself. "I now practice yoga and meditate for three hours every day and read as much metaphysical material as I can. With the awareness that I acquired, I know that with faith in the Creative Forces referred to in the Cayce material, everything will work out for the best. Feeling good about yourself and having a positive attitude is a valuable thing. Mine was lost for awhile, but it came back, and I will never lose it again."

It takes the brave kind of hope to face yourself in the solitude of a cell, yet Hal is doing it every day. He also has a new hope for his future because of a change in the federal sentencing guidelines and concludes, "I still hope for an early release. I am still optimistic about a change in the sentencing laws and feel that this experience has elevated me to a higher level of awareness. I thank God every day for the opportunity He has given me to improve my spiritual growth and development."

✳   ✳   ✳

Brave hope is by no means discriminatory. Anyone who is in need can reach inside and pull out a handful of hope. Much like Hal, Tina, a redhead from Boston, encountered hope one day when she took a long hard look in her own mirror.

She was in the grips of depression during a one-year separation from Brandon, the man whom she intended to marry. They had dated for two years and suddenly he announced that his feelings had changed and that he needed to see other people. Having no way of knowing whether the separation would be temporary or permanent, Tina felt almost powerless. "Almost" because she still possessed a small, brave hope from a feeling she had had shortly after they first met. "Perhaps this was the one true ESP experience of my life," Tina recalls. "It was a feeling, not a wishing, that he would be my husband. It was a knowing that he was THE ONE."

Now that he had announced his change of feelings, her "knowing" seemed totally illogical; however, she simply resolved to let time prove all things. His feelings had changed after what she calls two "idyllic" years. Though confused and dismayed, she also knew that he had to do what he had to do. She decided to quietly let him go. As time passed, she began to wrestle within herself and to question: "Would he come back? Is he gone for good? Would sticking around be a waste of time or should I move on with my life?"

Tina wallowed in depression, playing and replaying possible scenarios in her head. She started missing work, she lost weight, she even walked differently. Her only hope was that initial feeling she had had. Although she was deeply upset on the inside, she always tried to think of Brandon's best interest and let him go on his way without making a scene. Some would think that this response is true bravery, but no. Tina's true bravery had not yet arrived. She was yet to learn the difference between acting brave and being truly brave.

That whole year they were apart, Brandon never realized how upset she was because she put an enormous amount of energy into appearing calm and compassionate around him. She kept a journal, where she wrote down her doubts— her fears about making a terrible mistake and about wasting time on someone who might never be her husband.

One day, for no particular reason, Tina decided to review

what she had written throughout the entire distressing year. At that moment, brave hope pointed a trumpet at her heart and sounded. Suddenly, in reading what she'd written in her journal, she could see a very clear-cut theme to all those words. All her writing was about *her* life, not Brandon's. Her journal clearly revealed in her own hand the need for a change in *her* attitude, not his. She suddenly knew she had been writing about herself, not him. Revelations were galloping into her mind, like a charging cavalry. She realized that her entire journal was a reflection of her own feelings of stagnation and that she had to take action. She had to live her own life instead of waiting for someone else to live it for her!

By the end of the day, Tina had resolved to get on with her life. She decided that she no longer needed anyone else to make her happy. Things might work out with him or they might not, but she would no longer worry about it. She would live her life the best she could, as fully as she could, and hope for the best. To her amazement, the very next day, Brandon called. Within a month they were engaged. Now happily married, Tina still believes that Brandon didn't come back until she didn't need him to come back.

She credits her instinctive knowing that he was THE ONE as the thread of hope that kept her involved from the beginning. But when the brave side of hope encouraged her to examine herself and to have the courage she would need to take back her life, she became truly brave. "From that moment of realization on," Tina says, "I bubbled with real hope, excitement, and relief!"

❋   ❋   ❋

Sometimes brave hope is wrapped in patience. It has no ticker-tape parade, it gives no great revelations or profound solutions. Instead, like a brave friend sitting quietly with you in a waiting room, hope simply stays with you to keep your spirits up while you wait for whatever happens next.

Jenny is waiting. Although she is thirty and on the lean side of her future, she says she "still" has hope. Trim and practical, she describes her situation: "I'm stuck in a job I don't like, in the military, and with no one special to share my life. Yet, I have faith that something great will happen! I will get out of the military and be able to find work as a civilian and I won't starve to death." Though she is waiting, Jenny is not the least bit passive. She's working diligently on her education and on improving her computer skills. She wants to eventually have a career in the computer field. She also has hope that someday she will find someone with whom she is compatible enough to share the rest of their lives together.

So far, the magic hasn't happened with either a job or a mate, but she says, "I still keep hoping . . . about two years ago a psychic told me that my new life would not begin until I am about thirty-four. Until then, I just keep waiting, working, studying, and hoping." She hasn't much longer to wait, and when it happens, no matter what happens, Jenny will be ready. She hasn't been alone in all her preparations and she hasn't wasted a moment's time. Brave hope has been with her, quietly cheering her on.

✳   ✳   ✳

Mark also needed a refill of hope. He needed help in healing his emotional wounds and making his dreams come true. Mark had just gotten divorced and had moved out of the house he had shared with his three-year-old daughter, Amy, and now ex-wife, Meredith. Now he was living alone in a one-room apartment.

By the end of his eleven-year marriage, Mark had become a mailman. But in the beginning of his life with Meredith, he had been a singer in a rock-and-roll band. Meredith had discouraged him from his musical career and for the past five years had even forbidden him to sing. Now, however, he no longer felt he needed to put his time and effort into his family. With his marriage at an end, he would get back to his music.

Although he could always sing well, he could never really play the guitar. He only knew the most basic chords, but he began to play to himself what little he could in his small apartment/room. Already feeling like a failure because of his divorce, he needed a boost of hope to even attempt to pick up a guitar. But it proved to be worth it.

His favorite music, the early rock-and-roll of Elvis Presley from 1955 and 1956, had been out of fashion for many years. Anyway, one afternoon Mark put on Elvis's records and tried to play along with them. He explains, "Imagine my joy when I found that those beloved songs were only three chords—and they were the three chords that I could play." He felt real hope for the first time in a long, long while.

Just as in Tina's life, brave hope is always there when someone is reclaiming something important. Mark was no exception. Brave hope was there keeping time with the tunes, and Mark was soon his old musical self. He was now feeling so brave that he actually dared to dream that he could write a song about his feelings and perform it—just like the old days. He had spent a lot of years being told by someone he loved not to sing. Yet, his new hope helped him to rehearse until he had the courage to try his music in public.

The time had come, and Mark was about to perform for the first time in many years. To make it even tougher, since he had always been part of a band, this was his first time as a solo player. Used to being in a group surrounded by other players, Mark needed brave hope to get through this challenge.

Well, he sang and played his new song at a nearby folk

club. The response was so positive that he actually got book-ings and began singing for audiences and getting paid. Hope inspired his bravery and sustained him so that he could make his own dreams come true.

Brave hope can push you in the right direction—even to center stage if that's where you belong. And when you've taken a wrong turn, it will point you in the right direction and send you safely home.

❊　❊　❊

Stanley was in Germany during World War II when he dis-covered a hidden reserve of hope. Like a giant cloak of protection, brave hope covered him and two other soldiers until they were safely back with their platoon.

Following D-day, an American combat command con-sisting of a platoon of light and medium tanks plus artillery were covering the roads heading toward Munich. Two com-panies of infantry were following along behind to "mop up." A jeep from headquarters, carrying Stanley and two other soldiers, made a wrong turn and ended up in a village that had not yet been captured. Because all the people were in the town's tiny air raid basement, the whole area seemed safely deserted.

Suddenly, the young Americans spotted three German soldiers hiding in the treeline. One of the lieutenants in Stanley's jeep spoke fluent German and he called out to the Germans, ordering them to surrender. They came out with their hands up. Stanley and his men interrogated them and found out that there were two German corps in the woods about ten miles away. The Germans told them that the corps wanted to surrender. Stanley put the three young pris-oners on the hood of the jeep and drove down to the woods. The two German corps surrendered, and the Americans marched them off to the allied lines.

Stanley recalls that the incident had created a tremendous risk to his life and those in the jeep with him. In the midst of war and surrender, the American men could have been led right into an ambush. Fortunately, the three German soldiers had been telling the truth. Yet, Stanley remembers himself bravely hoping that they would not be killed or betrayed by the young enemy soldiers while accepting their surrender in the woods. Hope was enlisted to keep him and his colleagues safe.

"We felt that God was with us," he says, "directing and protecting us. We became fearless in accomplishing the surrender and proceeded bravely down the road, joining the combat command that was advancing on Nuremberg and Munich. God watched over us and brought us back home to our loved ones."

✳ ✳ ✳

Brave hope answers every call, from the cry for a strong and silent ally to the need for a victorious, courageous hero. No matter what the range of requests, brave hope has a common trait. It is never, ever afraid. It is bold and brazen in the face of any challenge. Think back to some of your own moments that required brave hope. Have you ever been worried and close to despair, yet somehow felt you weren't afraid? Chances are that was your own source of hope cropping up to inspire your bravery. You'll always know when hope is emerging because the absence of fear means the presence of your own brave hope.

3
HOPE
IS CALM

*"Hope for me is a
trust in the future and
a confidence in myself."*

Lyn Wade of Boulder, Colorado

Hope can be a natural sedative, prescribed by our own needs to take the edge off our angst and dull our dread. Like sipping a cup of hot tea on a damp afternoon or like taking a slow, deep breath in spring, hope can be a secret resource to calm our anxiety, mollify our messes, and still our fiendish worries.

❄ ❄ ❄

Tim did not even recognize hope when it calmly spoke in his ear for the first time. He was forty-eight years old. His wife, Alice, a couple of years his junior, was in the hospital for heart surgery. The day before, the doctor had described the procedure to both of them. Tim had gone home and tried to busy himself with chores around the house. He was very upset, feeling helpless and frustrated. He walked aimlessly for hours in the back yard, full of worry about the way the surgery might turn out. Suddenly from out of nowhere he heard the words, "Everything will be all right."

Tim, a gentle man in a burly body, quickly looked around, but no one was there. Instantly, he describes being overcome by an "immediate peace and calmness." The feeling gave him a powerful hope that seemed to smooth out his nerves and quiet his fears. He did not realize at the time that it was his own hope that was reassuring him and taking care of him. "It has happened several times since then for different reasons," Tim relates, "and I now know what it is." So he easily recognizes the tranquil touch of calming hope whenever it arrives.

※ ※ ※

Martha is a widow in her early fifties, living outside Saginaw, Michigan, near the mouth of Lake Huron. Her first visit from this calming aspect of hope came shortly after a bitter cold snap had broken her water pipes and had almost broken her spirit. She was already feeling depressed because her husband had recently passed on. The void he had left behind in her life and her children's lives was sorely felt. Now she was faced with her first major home repair all alone.

She and her son had just returned from a week's Christmas visit to her mother's home in Missouri, a bleak homecoming for Martha. She dropped her son at his apartment and headed for home. As she walked into her empty house, feeling very sad and lonely, she realized that the water pipes over her bedroom ceiling had burst. Close to tears and with shoulders slumped, she headed for the kitchen wondering how it had happened, whom to call, and what to do first. She felt utterly alone and full of longing for her departed partner of thirty-some years. Then, she noticed a pile of notes on her washing machine that had been left by her neighbor Nel, whom Martha had asked to feed her cat while she was away.

She sat down at the table and started reading the little notes, trying to piece together what had happened. The morning Martha left, a sharp, cold wind was blowing off the lake out of the northeast, driving the temperature below zero. That afternoon, when Nel opened the door to feed the cat, she heard water running and ran to the phone to call another neighbor, Ruddie. Ruddie made a few calls, and men and women from Martha's church group and other church groups came out of nowhere to help. They shut off the main water source and moved her mattress and some of her furniture to a dry place. They even washed and dried her bedding—all this while Martha was 900 miles away.

When Martha arrived home, saw the mess, and found out what had been done, she recalls feeling "dumbfounded in a very thankful way." But there was still so much for her to do, she didn't have the faintest idea of how to go about it. Although she was truly grateful, she was, at the same time, feeling hopeless and completely overwhelmed. When she went to bed that night (on her couch), she prayed for help to cope with this disaster. Her fears were larger than the damage from the burst water pipe, however, and she added a prayer for the strength she now knew she would need to face the rest of her life without her husband's emotional support. "Oh, how I prayed," she recalls. "I felt totally unprepared for the future."

The next morning, a neighboring farmer knocked at her door. He said that he was passing her house on the way to his farm and, on an impulse, decided to swing his truck down her driveway to offer his help. He spent the rest of the

morning and part of the afternoon telling Martha exactly
what the insurance company would need on the list of
damages. He even took her into town to her insurance
agency, helped her report the whole mess, drove her back
to the house, then went over instructions on what to do
next.

As she sat on the floor listening to her neighbor go over
all the details she must now handle, Martha says she suddenly felt hope. She describes it as "a calming, sustaining
presence wrapping itself all the way around me. My mind
began to feel that God was watching over me with loving
care. I began to feel hope for the first time since I returned
home."

She flashed back to her prayers of the night before and
realized that she now had the answer to how she would continue her life without her husband's emotional support. As
the calmness made its way around her tired shoulders, she
suddenly knew that the kindness of her neighbors, friends,
and fellow church members had triggered her own reserve
of hope. In that moment of calm, Martha recognized her
own hope and the way it had been awakened by the supportive people surrounding her.

One month later, she had begun to slip back into some of
her old loneliness when she felt that same warm, calming
hope rising inside her again. This time it was triggered by
the view from her window. "On a glorious, dazzling morning when I was driving home from town, the sun shone
down out of an intensely blue sky—its rays falling like a
thousand glistening rainbows—and I knew everything
would fall into place once more . . . I knew that God is in His
heaven and all's well with the world."

*　*　*

Calm hope belongs to all of us, no matter at what age or

stage of life we are. It can be awakened through friends, at churches, even on college campuses—as with this story from Rosemary. Like most college students, Rosemary had a sense of self-worth that was still being determined by her peers instead of by her own soul. Making top grades and being a successful leader had been her way of gaining approval in high school. Now, however, in her upstate New York college she used her ability to attract boys as a way of gaining the admiration of her friends. Yet, when Rosemary used deception against her roommate Peggy, her fragile world of peer approval completely collapsed.

Although she was never shy with boys, no one knew how quiet Rosemary really was around her female peers because she covered up so well her feelings of inadequacy. Her pretty and pert roommate Peggy, however, was more comfortable with girls and always felt nervous around boys. Consequently, the two roommates seemed to complement each other. During their sophomore year in college, Peggy started dating a handsome senior who was a real catch on campus. His name was Carl. Although she really liked Carl, Peggy didn't know how to behave around him, so Rosemary served as her confidant and adviser on how to keep him interested. Her advice worked well because Peggy dated Carl for the rest of the school year.

That summer Peggy went home, but Carl and Rosemary both stayed on campus to attend summer school. They had, of course, become friends, so they played some tennis together and shared a few other campus activities. Quite unintentionally, they fell in love. Rosemary felt so guilty about this turn of events that she insisted they keep their feelings a secret. She just couldn't bear to be the one who took away the boyfriend she had worked so hard to help Peggy keep. Carl reluctantly went along with Rosemary's secrecy because, if he didn't, she threatened to end the relationship with him completely. Rosemary planned to break the news gently to Peggy when the time was right. They were all so young, and she just didn't know what else to do.

Carl graduated at the end of that summer and was drafted into military service. That fall he wrote to Peggy openly and to Rosemary secretly. When he came to campus, he dated only Peggy, but continued to protest to Rosemary about the deception. However, Rosemary couldn't seem to find a way to tell her roommate.

Peggy finally learned the truth from someone else and, when she did, she was convinced that Rosemary's deception was an insult rather than the kindness that had been intended. She was deeply hurt and embarrassed and, of course, told all their girlfriends what an insincere person Rosemary was. Suddenly Rosemary's worst fears were realized: She found herself friendless.

The effect of losing all her friends in one afternoon was devastating. She managed to carry on with school for a day or two and sought counseling with a teacher, but nothing helped. She tossed and turned through a third sleepless night in deep worry. In the most dark, desperate hours of the night some helpful thoughts quietly and carefully began to flow into her mind. They were thoughts from Ralph Waldo Emerson's essay "Self-Reliance," which Rosemary was studying in American literature. Those thoughts gradually became her own as she carefully reviewed her life up to that point. Slowly her depression was replaced by hope. "I was filled with a calm assurance and an inner joy," Rosemary relates. "By morning I was radiant with hope, peace, and joy. I had undergone a total change in consciousness."

She shook her sleeping roommate to wake her up and excitedly explained to Peggy her new understanding of why she had acted the way she did. Then she asked her for forgiveness. Peggy was a bit puzzled by Rosemary's glorious revelation, but she was now convinced of her roommate's sincerity and forgave her for the deception. Word passed quickly through the campus grapevine, and all was soon well again. It took some time for Peggy to sort out her feelings connected with Carl. She would have to come to the realization that he didn't love her the way he did Rosemary. But her first step in sorting out all her emotions came from forgiving her roommate for the deception.

Rosemary concludes, "My hope was born out of a deep hopelessness, and there is a very happy ending. The young man in the story has been my beloved husband for thirty-seven years." Rosemary's pre-dawn awakening of peaceful hope changed her life forever. It gently nudged her away from misery and toward self-esteem.

✳ ✳ ✳

Calm hope emerged for another woman in the evening hours, late at night, and much later in her life. For Dana, it was in the form of a peace-giving dream. Dana's father had died quickly. Within one month after his diagnosis of cancer of the liver, he was gone. No one was emotionally prepared for his death, least of all Dana, who was at the time a young mom, deeply involved with the blossoming side of life. She was going to need a reminder of her own power of hope.

Dana had not invested much into her relationship with her father. Her life was full of her own young children, a husband, and a career. Consequently, at the time of her father's sudden death, she felt that she had missed the chance to really know him. She remembered him only through a child's eyes. She felt anxious—as if she had been cheated out of an adult opportunity to bond with her dad.

The years have passed since his death. Now Dana, who is forty-three, wanted to understand her father and what he had gone through in his life. Her children have since grown and are busy with their lives. She was feeling disappointed because this should have been the time to actually "social-ize" with her father. Then one night she had a dream about him. Not a dream of the past, but a dream of the present where she is a grown woman and he an old man. Then more dreams of him came—about visits, picnics, and walks in the park. In every dream, Dana and her father would talk. The dreams began to give her hope that she was finally getting to know her long, lost parent.

Though she can't remember the details of her recurring dreams, she always wakes up feeling close to her father. She can recall his face, his characteristics, and mannerisms. "It's as if I am getting a second chance—knowing and learning and just being with him as an adult. I feel a hopefulness from these dreams, knowing that I have not lost contact with my father and that I never will."

* * *

A calming hope can appear anywhere. For a woman named Arlene, hope appeared when she was wide awake. It was a time in her life when it was vitally important that she remain calm, and hope helped her to keep composed under pressure.

At forty-eight, Arlene decided to return to college to complete a master's degree she had started many years earlier. The only requirement she needed to finish her degree was her master's project. Several years before, when she was working on that same degree, Arlene, for some reason, had simply given up and never invested another ounce of effort in her project. Lately, however, after reviewing her transcripts, she realized how close she was to obtaining her degree. She decided to "go for it"—all the way. This time she increased her chances of success by soliciting the aid of her friends who regularly joined with her in prayer. Together they devised a scriptural prescription for success that included affirmations which she began to read daily.

Arlene confidently went about the business of designing her project and doing the necessary research. It was not easy; however, she finally got the report finished and handed it in. Relieved to be through, she immediately felt thankful, knowing that she had put forth her best energy and had been sincere in her prayer work.

When she finally received her letter from the committee, she opened it, knowing that she had passed. Instead, the letter informed her that she had *not* passed. Although she was shocked and saddened, it was only a brief response. She explains, "In my bones I believed that the light of God never fails and that I had earnestly called forth that light. I was working with the universe, so how could there be a mistake?"

She made a call to the department head to arrange an appointment in order to discuss a possible misunderstanding. Convinced that a mistake had been made, she in the meantime kept telling herself and others that she had passed—but the committee didn't know it yet. On the date of the appointment she went in feeling victorious. As she parked her car on the campus parking lot, she uttered a prayer and stated one of her most precious affirmations: "Almighty God's presence goes before me making easy and instant and perfect my way." She immediately felt cool headed and poised.

When she arrived in his wooden-walled office, he was on the telephone. From his worn leather chair he motioned for her to sit down. Arlene waited patiently for him to finish his conversation. The longer he spoke, the more her confidence wavered; inside she began to feel fear. This appointment was the culmination of all her efforts, and she was starting to doubt herself. Suddenly, she was filled with a calming hope and a feeling that she should just sit still and wait. Something seemed to tell her, "Don't talk, don't try to prove anything, don't be confrontational, just sit there. It will all be O.K." She took a long, silent, deep breath.

Finally the chairman hung up the phone and said, "Welcome, Mrs. Williams. Your paper was excellent." Arlene nodded and waited stoically to hear why an "excellent paper" had not passed. He then told her how the committee was formed by three members, one of whom had refused to accept a certain portion of her paper. With a renewed hope slowly rising to her consciousness, Arlene says that she was able to simply wait, peacefully watching him. After a short pause, he said, "Let's call it a pass."

"My heart leaped for joy," Arlene recalls. "I thanked the chairman and left his office in a spirit of deepest gratitude and a great confirmation for hope and faith." Her calm hope had surfaced in the chairman's office when she had begun to doubt herself—like a gentle hand on her arm assuring her that everything would be all right and reminding her that she had done her work—now it was time to let go. She adds that this successful experience has made her more keenly aware of how important it is to keep her own ego out of the way and just feel the comfort of her own hope.

❋ ❋ ❋

Three weeks after Penny had given birth to her second son, her mother-in-law Barbra, whom she dearly loved, suffered a ruptured varicose vein in her esophagus. It was a terrible shock and loss when Barbra was taken to the hospital because she had been visiting Penny almost daily. Now Penny felt abandoned and alone in addition to being worried about Barbra's health. To make matters worse, she had a bad cold and wasn't even able to visit her mother-in-law in the hospital.

Ten days later, nearly sick with worry for her wonderful

in-law, Penny was informed by the doctors that Barbra wouldn't make it. Her bad cold didn't matter to her now after hearing this news—nothing was going to stop her from going to see Barbra. She got a sitter for her children and drove straight to the local hospital in northern Illinois where Barbra was being treated. When Penny arrived, she found that Barbra was unable to talk. There were tubes everywhere, and Barbra had to ration her energy just to breathe. All Penny could do was stroke her forehead the way Barbra had done for Penny whenever she was ill. Penny wanted to say something to her but couldn't get her voice to work either. Three days later Barbra died.

It was Penny's first adult experience with the death of someone so close. She was severely shaken, overwhelmed with grief and with a terrible anxiety about Barbra's fate. Penny had been raised in a Christian fundamentalist church. Even though she had been reading some material about life after death (on the sly), she just wasn't sure what would happen to Barbra now.

Barbra had been a very talented musician long before she and Penny had first met. She had loved life and children, but had suffered through an unfortunate marriage and a manic-depressive condition. Both had contributed to her developing alcoholism and an eventual nervous breakdown. She had been hospitalized for years before Penny knew her. By the time Penny came into the family, however, Barbra was well enough to live at home with the help of tranquilizers and, unfortunately, a continuation of alcohol use.

Penny had loved Barbra deeply and felt that her mother-in-law had never had a chance to live and do what she had entered life to do. The viewing at the local funeral home was agony for her. She couldn't look at Barbra's closed eyes and struggled to open her own eyes as wide as possible to stop the tears—which came anyway. She was so upset that she couldn't even pray.

Some nights later Penny had a dream. In the dream she and her father-in-law were sitting in Barbra's living room playing bridge. Barbra slowly materialized behind her husband and placed her hand on his shoulder. At first she was ghostlike but slowly gained substance until she looked real. Barbra was laughing and joyful and had on her favorite bright-colored shorts and blouse. She stood there just for a moment and then faded away.

When Penny woke up, her fear and anxiety had dissolved just like the image of her mother-in-law. She knew that Barbra was well and much happier than she'd ever been in this lifetime. Penny was truly calm for the first time in a long while. She also began to really understand what the books she had been reading had said about life after death. Having seen Barbra in the dream reassured her. It gave her hope to know that we continue on after leaving the body behind at the time of death.

Penny's own father died seven years later. Again she grieved, but this time she was able to calmly look at his body. With affection, she knew he was probably watching them all and enjoying his funeral. Later, Penny's mother suggested that the whole family sing some of his favorite hymns and asked the organist to play Handel's "Hallelujah Chorus" for the postlude. Penny states, "What an incredible difference knowledge and having hope can make!"

✳ ✳ ✳

Anyone can tap into his or her own resources of calm hope just like Peggy or Tim or Martha did. It doesn't have to be invited because of an emergency. It can be a part of your daily routine. Somewhere between brushing your teeth in the morning and setting your alarm clock at night, stop for a moment, close your eyes, take a few deep breaths, and focus on feeling hopeful. Feel hopeful that you will get through the day peacefully, regardless of what challenges your boss may have for you or what conflict your co-workers may tempt you with. If the school nurse calls to tell you your child is sick, feel hopeful that you will be able to leave work without guilt or resentment to take care of him or her. You can make sure your hope supply is ready to use at a moment's notice by recognizing the signals and symbols that emerge, that remind you to sit still, take a deep breath, and be calm. With a little bit of effort and within a short amount of time, you will have incorporated calm hope into your daily life style. You will have given yourself the greatest gift of all—you will have created for yourself the habit of hope.

4

HOPE

IS CONTAGIOUS

"By your very step,
by your very look, by your very word,
create hope in the hearts,
minds, and lives of others."

Based on Edgar Cayce Reading 5749-13

Hope is easily transmittable. You can become hopeful from shaking hands with someone who is hopeful, from hearing someone laugh or seeing another smile. By just standing close to a person who is hopeful you can begin to feel hopefulness dissolving your doubts. Warning: hopefulness can be easily spread. Direct contact is not necessary to catch the essence of hope. It is transmitted by touch, it is airborne, and it is highly contagious!

* * *

One cold, still night in December, Roslyn received a

phone call that her younger brother Sam along with his wife, Marion, had been in a car accident. They were hit from behind by a drunk driver who was speeding over 100 miles per hour. On this particular night, for some unknown reason, Roslyn had decided to stay home from her usual karate lesson. She recalls that she had not missed a Thursday lesson in two-and-one-half years because of her dedication to the training. Yet on that evening, she felt restless and decided at the last minute to stay home. Consequently, she was home alone when the call came.

During that time of her life she was already grieving for her parents who had died four months apart during the previous year and "the grieving was still too real for me." Now, she was told over the phone that her brother was also dead. "The death of Sam was perhaps the greatest pain I had yet to experience," explains Roslyn. "Being extremely close as children, we had even become more dependent upon each other following the deaths of our parents."

All Roslyn knew about the crash was that Marion had been driving. The severity of Marion's injuries would not be known until later. Roslyn only knew that her sister-in-law was alive and had been flown to Pittsburgh after a two-hour rescue attempt to get her out of the car. Marion was already in surgery when the call came to Roslyn about Sam. The following day, she and her older brother Walt (all who remained of the Taylor family) made the journey to the site of the accident to speak with the police and then to see Marion. Roslyn dreaded the encounter.

The shock of seeing the crumpled car was disheartening. The motor, steering wheel, and dashboard were jammed into the front seat. The roof, doors, and what was left of the windshield had been cut away to remove the passengers. As she gazed at this sight, Roslyn could visualize the impact on their bodies. Her career of working in emergency rooms had given her enough images of what this scene must have looked like only yesterday.

As she stared at the mutilated car, Roslyn's thoughts were filled with Sam. "How long after the impact had he lived? Did he know he was dying? Is his soul still waiting here, disoriented from the shock? Does he realize how much I loved and needed him? Is he with Mom and Dad? And what about Marion?" From the look of it, Roslyn imagined her sister-in-law with a cut face, fractured sternum, broken legs and arms. "Is she conscious, is she permanently disabled, does she know that Sam died and she didn't?"

When Roslyn and Walt arrived at the hospital, Roslyn's legs were weak and unstable. With her heart pounding in her throat, she felt anxious about seeing Marion. She was sure there was no hope because this tragic accident had already claimed her brother's life and probably severely injured her sister-in-law. Outside the hospital room, Roslyn stopped, took several deep breaths to give herself strength, and prepared herself for whatever state Marion would be in, physically or emotionally. As she entered the room, Marion was sitting up in bed, her arm bandaged and in a metal fracture cast. Astonishingly, there was a white glow radiating from her, and Roslyn froze in disbelief as she noted that there was not a mark on her! No bruises, no fractured sternum. Her legs were intact, without a nick or scratch. Evidently on impact Marion had reached out for her husband and had almost crushed her wrist. Even though the engine was in her lap, there was not a mark on the rest of her body. Roslyn realized at that moment that she was witnessing a miracle—a living miracle. She saw the glow, the unbelievable radiance around Marion and burst into tears. Marion was alive, conscious, though severely sad, and except for her wrist, untouched.

"I experienced hope for the first time in my life that day," Roslyn recounts. "They had three children safe at home and their mother was spared. Despite the pain inside of me, I felt Marion's hope. I saw the crashed car and heard the account of how they had cut her free from the engine. I went to Marion and touched her face. I looked at her legs and told her, 'You are a miracle.'"

The hope emanating from Marion and the fact that she was alive and virtually unmarred by the accident had reawakened Roslyn's own hope. Her grief, layered upon grief, had been eased by one sole survivor.

※ ※ ※

For a woman named Irene, her dwindling hope was renewed by the birth of her daughter, Jean Marie. Jean Marie was conceived when Irene and her husband had reunited after a six-month separation. Previously, because of the destructive effects of drugs and alcohol, they had lost all their material possessions, and their oldest daughter Patty was staying with other members of the family because of their separation.

With their lives and their marriage nearly destroyed, Irene and her husband had left Patty behind in Kansas to start their lives over again in Texas. In Texas, however, Irene remembers, they were literally eating from store dumpsters to stay alive. "A baby on the way seemed too much for us to bear financially. I even hit myself in the stomach to try and rid myself of the 'problem,' and I asked my relatives for money for an abortion." She had no hope for herself, her future, or the future of the baby she was carrying.

No money came, and by the fourth month Irene herself was no longer considering an abortion. She realized that this baby was a part of her and would be born somehow, even though she knew from past experience that she would require a Caesarean section. Irene applied for Medicaid, was approved, and Jean Marie's birth was a success. Irene states that when Jean Marie came into the world she brought hope with her. She still marvels at the power of the infectiousness of that hope that her new baby triggered in her. The baby's birth reminded her that we all can start new every day. Each day can be our first day—full of innocence and anticipation.

Irene's story moves swiftly to the present. "I'm now a devoted mother, my husband has a steady job. We are both clean, sober, and financially O.K. I work three days a week, and we have a beautiful, strong, stubborn little girl who gives me hope every day. Patty is with us again, and both children are wonderful, God-loving, little people who give me strength to carry on in the midst of conflict and chaos in everyday problems."

Jean Marie's birth acted as the trigger of contagious hope for her mother. Irene rocked, fed, and nurtured her infant—and her own growing hope. She then began to hope for a better life, a reunion with Patty, and a job for her husband—all the things she never dared hope for before. Her hope thrived just like her child, and it spread to other areas of her life. We can learn from Irene. We can nurture and feed hope in ourselves and pass it on to others. We can do this by remembering that hope takes attention and effort in order for it to rise and blossom. Irene has a constant reminder that she almost denied her baby a chance to live and grow. We can remind ourselves daily to never deprive our own hope the chance to develop within us.

❋   ❋   ❋

Gill caught hope at college. He was enrolled in graduate studies in his chosen field, yet he was feeling at odds with the faculty and fellow students at the elite institution he had chosen. He explains, "My different background and my experiences left me bitter about what I perceived as squandering, rich students. Additionally, my own creative efforts were not encouraged by my professors because they viewed my work differently than I did." Consequently, Gill was feeling totally hopeless about his situation.

By chance, he attended a theatrical performance produced by a Professor Hume, whom he admired because of his ability to incorporate spirituality into his performances. Gill wrote a paper on his admired teacher's work. When Dr. Hume read it, he immediately took Gill under his wing. Gill says of him, "Because he had high hopes for me, he fostered my own personal and professional development and aided me in overcoming obstacles. I believe he was brought into my life by God. Professor Hume has since passed on, yet his legacy is the inspiration left to countless artists by his example. The thread of hope he wove into the fabric of my life is one made of knowledge, intuition, and love."

Today, whenever Gill feels down or incapable of any creative effort, he thinks of his old teacher's hope in him and moves on. By recalling Professor Hume's hopefulness, Gill can then feel his own hopeful energy around him that energizes his current career as a screenwriter. Despite his negative feelings about the school, the other students, and the other professors in his youth, Gill caught a good dose of hopefulness in a place where he least expected it.

✳ ✳ ✳

Emily caught hope in the same way as Irene, Roslyn, and Gill. Each was sure that conditions were hopeless and that they were immune to hope, but they caught hope anyway from someone who touched their lives.

Emily recounts her situation: "It's odd. I gained hope after I had lost all hope. I come from a dysfunctional family. I was widowed at age twenty-six, and I had been in counseling for a few years trying to find my way out of a long dark tunnel." Already feeling vulnerable about the future, Emily learned that her best friend and husband were splitting up. She viewed their perfect relationship as the last bastion of hope—a relationship that worked. For her, the split-up was the last straw.

For several years Emily had told her counselor that she saw no reason to continue to fight to have a happier life, and the separation of her role-model friends finally convinced her she had been right. She simply gave up trying to live or die. Death would come whether she felt better or not. So she was just going to watch and wait. It no longer mattered to her. Without hope, she simply quit trying.

Shortly before she had heard about the divorce of her friend, Emily had signed up for a parapsychology class being taught at the local community college. Disgruntled and depressed, she went to class anyway and now says, "The first night of class was the end and the beginning for me." Her teacher talked about things that Emily had always kept secret in her heart. She had told no one but her late husband of her deep spiritual beliefs. Her beliefs were never middle of the road, and she had had experiences that could not be explained away easily. Yet her new teacher understood.

Several times her instructor, a healthy carrier of hope, looked Emily straight in the eyes and said things that she had quietly thought about—thoughts that had previously made her feel isolated for so many years. Now the teacher's words were flying to her and spreading hope all through her body. She was exposed to her teacher's hope and she caught it.

The words reached her heart so deeply that "they touched a place that had never been touched. In that moment a light was lit. Those words, spoken out loud with love, took away my darkness. I saw hope being born inside of me for the first time since I lost my husband. I have been able to clear each hurdle since that day. I released my pain and anger about my husband and opened my heart to God and the Light."

* * *

Merril was in his late forties when he caught his first serious case of hope; now he wants to spread it to others. He was hit by a truck that had run a red light while he was crossing a street in New York City. For three months, he lay in a coma as the doctors tried to convince his son Nicholas that he would not live. Yet Nicholas would not give up hope.

Merril knows this because, he says, even in a coma he was aware of the presence of others, especially of Nicholas, by his bedside. He could feel how hard Nicholas was fighting for him and he could feel his son's hope for breaking through the veil that separated them.

"The great love and hope of Nicholas pulled me through. Now, I am very much alive, talking, walking, and staying busy with three jobs. I am very much committed to the idea of spending the rest of my life counseling others about the importance of hope. I am firmly convinced that the philosopher Soren Kierkegaard was right when he suggested that the only unforgivable sin is that of despair." Thanks to Nicholas, Merril now has a contagious hope of his own to use and to share with others.

* * *

This next story is a little different from the others. Shawna caught hope, but she caught it at the young age of sixteen and, not only that, she caught it because of someone else's pain. As she explains it, "I'm not sure if you'd call this an experience involving hope, but it was a light at the end of a very dark tunnel."

Shawna's father died suddenly of a heart attack and, being "Daddy's little girl," it threw her into one of the darkest, most desolate times in her young life. Her parents had divorced about three years before and the times spent with her dad had become very special. They never missed a weekend together. So the news of his death sent her plunging downward and her world began falling in on top of her. She felt abandoned and cheated. "No one has ever had this happen to them," Shawna thought. She shut herself off from everyone, refusing to talk or eat or participate in anything. She just wanted to be left alone in her misery. To this day, she doesn't really know how long this darkness persisted. "It just seemed to go on forever."

Three months before his death, her father had remarried. One day it dawned on Shawna that she had forgotten all about her stepmother—a woman now a widow who had quit her job in another state, leaving family and friends behind to start a new life with her new husband. At that moment, she began seeing this tragedy through her stepmother's pain. When she started thinking that at least she (Shawna) had sixteen years of memories and good times, she felt the darkness begin to lift, and her hopes for a happy life were once again illuminated.

She discovered that the more she focused on her stepmother's suffering, the more she began to realize what treasures she did have—like her health and her family and friends close by. The joy of life started to flow again. Shawna comments, "Maybe when we stop and look around us, we see things differently—seeing someone else's pain and really feeling for them—then we can find hope in the good parts of our lives and the memories of loved ones we will always have."

Since the moment she caught hope from someone else's pain, Shawna says, "This experience has helped me to always try to put myself in another person's shoes—see it from that person's perspective. That means trying to find the good side of a bad situation. Now when I'm trying to overcome shyness and self-consciousness, I try empathizing with the other person's nervousness or fearfulness instead of my own. It works."

* * *

Brooke found hope from a less obvious source. Not from a relative or a teacher, but from an unexpected visit. One night her sister called saying that Brooke's dearest friend, Andrew, had died. Her sister was crying uncontrollably throughout the phone call, but Brooke confidently told her not to cry, that Andrew was at peace. Her sister was surprised, even shocked, that Brooke wasn't outwardly upset about his passing.

The funeral was scheduled for next Saturday, and Brooke made travel arrangements to attend it. For her, the days before the funeral were peaceful. Family members and friends were in shock. They were sad and stricken with grief, but Brooke did not cry even one tear. Once at the funeral, however, she did weep. She saw Andrew's two natural sons and a grandson, whom he had just adopted. It was truly sad. His mother and a host of relatives and friends were choking with sorrow. Though Brooke had finally cried, it was not one of those cleansing, deep cries that releases your true feelings. Two days later, she arrived back home, still not really feeling the loss of her dearest friend. Everyone else—her family, his family, and his friends—were all still in shock and feeling bitter and sad.

The next morning Brooke woke up thinking about Andrew and his zest for life, the plans he had made for the future with the woman he loved and for his grandson. She thought about how good and beautiful this man had been as a human being. She remembered the people he helped. Finally she began to cry. This time she wept uncontrollably with great sobs and moans of regret. "No one could stop me," she recalls. "Me, the one who believed in life after death! I deeply missed him. I realized how good he had been to so many people. I realized that I loved him so very much. My mother worried about me because for two days I didn't eat, and I could not stop crying.

"Then, I went upstairs to my room. I prayed. I needed to know desperately if there is life after death. I called for him and he came. Something grabbed my hand and touched my eye, my lips, and my heart. And it said, not with a voice, but with a feeling through me: 'I love you. I am happy. I would rather be here than there.' This man who loved life, who had just adopted his grandson, and who had left a host of family and friends behind said that he was happy and would rather be there! He said, 'There is life after life. There is hope.' "

Brooke still gets visits from Andrew. Each time he comes he brings a new dose of hope. Not only can hope be transmitted from those closest to us, it can also travel from the other side of life and infect us here with hopefulness.

✻ ✻ ✻

April also caught hope from that world beyond which we sometimes can see, taste, feel, and smell. She discovered that hope was communicable from a psychic—a courier of hope from the other side. She explains, "When my husband of eighteen years, the father of our four children, told me that he had been having an affair with someone else and was in love with this other woman, my life lost its solid footing."

Unfortunately, April believed that it was her fault. In fact, she was sure she hadn't done enough, been pleasing enough, or acted as she was supposed to act toward him. She was convinced that she was a complete failure. The future, even the next day, seemed like a chaotic fog; she felt lost and she had no hope.

At the urging of a friend who offered to pay half the fee, April went to an intuitive psychic, who spoke with authority and said to April, "Where you are is perfect for you now. It is as if you have been living with someone in the first grade—being in the first grade is fine, but it is time for you to move on. You will not recognize yourself in five years."

April felt as if the heavens had opened. This new perspective awakened her hope and gave her what she needed to turn herself around and look forward again. She began to look at herself without judging. She looked directly in the mirror at herself and asked, "Who is this person who is no longer her husband's right arm? Where am I? How can I start fresh?"

With her newly caught hope, April began to attack her old attitudes. Making a complete change, she enrolled in an acupuncture school and even had the courage to have a friend paint her nude so that she would be able to see her body from a distance. She began talking about ideas that interested her, developing friends who liked to talk about the same things. She took workshops designed to find out some of her weaknesses and what she could do about them.

She adds, "Although it wasn't all fun, it was definitely worthwhile. Little by little a wonderful new person began to emerge—me! I am now an acupuncturist and an acupuncture teacher, both of which I love doing. I use them as points of departure for further exploration. Two of my children have left the nest; the other two are normally happy with their lives. More and more, I am exploring what healing really means."

* * *

Contagious hope can come from many sources. It can

come from other people's joys and other people's pain. It can even come from other worlds. In this world, however, we often spend too much time trying not to catch what other people have. We are cautioned to protect ourselves from contact. But, in the case of hope, the rules are reversed. Where hope is involved, go on out there and catch a case of hope.

5

HOPE
IS DETERMINED

*"Hope is a clear,
soft, powerful, steady
feeling that will not pass."*

William Munns of Seattle, Washington

Hope can be like background music in your life, quietly and constantly providing the backbeat for success and strength. It doesn't interfere with the flow of life; it merely takes out the guesswork. For those who know their own power of determined hope, they don't need to re-invite it into their lives because it's always there—they only need to turn up its volume.

* * *

In a hospital lobby in Peoria, during the unfriendly hours before dawn, a family was waiting for the results of a loved one's surgery. It was a long, hard operation. The surgeon was discouraged, not so much by the time required for the surgery, but by the rising temperature that was now threatening the recovery of his sixty-seven-year-old patient. "It was a difficult surgery due to the infection, and I don't see how he can make it through the night," said the fatigued surgeon to the family. "His temperature is already 102 degrees."

Jill was not afraid about her father's scorching temperature. Instead of listening to the doctor, she was reviewing a conversation that she had had with her father the night before. As she was leaving the hospital that night, her father Ned said, "So long. I'll be seeing you." Because surgery was scheduled for 7:00 a.m., Jill said she would be there by 6:00. She got to the hospital late and missed seeing him. Now, standing in the cold, clean lobby, Jill refused to believe that her father would die because, after all, he had told her he would be seeing her.

The next day the doctor came and went from Room 208 shaking his head and saying, "He won't make it through the night. There's no way he can survive a temperature of 107 degrees." By the second evening, Sister Pius, the nurse on duty, asked Jill not to come to her dad's room—it would only worry her. She promised to call Jill if there was any change. Jill obliged Sister Pius and drove to her parents' house. When she arrived, she found her mother, brothers, and sisters sitting at the kitchen table planning Ned's funeral. Jill was disgusted and went storming out into the night to talk to God.

It was an icy night with a full moon. Crisp new snow sparkled in the twenty-one-below-zero air. Jill walked and prayed and instinctively knew that God was listening. She was turning up the volume on her hope. She had never given up hope about her father, but too many people were doubting. Now she needed some reassurance. With determination, she looked up at the sky and said, "God, if You will let my father live this time, I will never ask for him to live again."

In an instant it seemed that all of heaven opened up and a distinctive and powerful voice said, "Peace be unto you." Jill felt immediately at peace, replenished with a warm unfaltering hope. She returned to the hospital and sat on the stairway across from Room 208 for the rest of that night.

As the sun filled the morning of the fifth day, Jill was pondering the wonders of God and His power of keeping her father alive. She suddenly heard footsteps coming down the hall from the chapel. The nurse who sat at a desk near her father's door looked toward the sound of those footsteps at the new nurse named Sister Sarah and motioned her into Ned's room. A few seconds later Sister Sarah came through the door, walked up to Jill, and said, "Would you like to help me change your father's bed? His fever is broken."

Both Jill and the nurse cried tears of gratitude all day as they changed Ned's bed and fed him crushed ice to heal his split and bleeding lips and tongue. Though he did not recognize anyone, Jill steadfastly searched his precious face—so swollen he hardly looked human. Some time later, the nurse at the desk told Jill that Sister Sarah had not left her father's side for two days except to go to the chapel. And the doctor simply shook his head and said, "St. Peter just threw Ned's crown in the corner."

Jill's father lived for sixteen more years, completely recovered from the sizzling fever he had survived. Everyone was surprised except Jill. Although she had had a few doubting moments, she was never astonished that her father recovered. She possessed the dogged, determined hope that would allow nothing but recovery to happen to him.

✳ ✳ ✳

Across the ocean is a case of determined hope that is still making an Italian doctor shake his head in disbelief. While twin sisters, Connie and Maria, were on holiday in London, their ninety-four-year-old Grandmother Lia back home in Italy had broken her thigh bone.

The same day that the sisters returned home from London, their grandmother was discharged from the hospital. It seems there was nothing more that could be done for the hip because she was too old for an operation. All the doctor could give her were high doses of painkillers. Consequently, she was sleeping all the time and would eat very little. When the granddaughters first saw their grandmother, they believed she was in fact dying from the hospital visit, not from the broken bone.

They learned that, while in the hospital, Lia had been fitted for a brace so that her hip would not move. She had to wear it all the time—even while sleeping. Within that month in the hospital, however, she had developed gangrene in her foot and halfway up her leg to her knee. She also had developed a huge ulcerous sore on her back from lying down so much and was starting to get erythema (redness) from the medicine. Connie and Maria could not remember Lia's ever taking any medicine. They did remember, however, that Lia always said, "Doctors are good only for killing you" and "The errors of the doctors are covered by the earth."

As soon as they had considered the extent of Lia's complications, the sisters went to work, determined to restore their grandmother's health. The first thing they did was throw away all the pills. They removed the brace and never put it back on again. Instead they used pillows to keep her leg straight.

With the help of their mother and aunt, they massaged Lia's decaying foot and leg four times a day with corn oil.

The erythema had spread all over her body except for her fragile face. Grandma herself told them to wash her with a soap that had a high soda content. That ancient village remedy made the erythema dry up right away.

In three months Lia could stand up and walk a few steps to her wheelchair and sit down with help. Within six months of her fall, she was walking again by herself. As of 1992, Connie and Maria's grandmother was ninety-seven years old and in perfect health. And the doctor still doesn't believe it! When he sees her out walking, he greets her and walks away shaking his head increduously.

Like anyone else who is determined in their hope, the granddaughters were committed to restoring Lia's health and they succeeded. There is little spontaneity with determined hope. You must simply decide on the desired result, and then take the steps to accomplish it.

*   *   *

For Elan, a young man working for Air Canada, hope stayed with him for two solid years, building his self-esteem and quietly keeping him on track. He had developed an interest in meteorology. Hoping to combine his new interest with his present job, he inquired through the Department of Transportation about a career as a weather forecaster. He was informed that there were many obstacles, not the least of which was the necessity for him to study advanced mathematics. Still, he was determined to put his interest in meteorology to good use.

Since he was already working for the airline, a friend suggested that he apply for a job as a flight dispatcher. As a dispatcher, he would still need to know about meteorology but not as much as a weather forecaster; he wouldn't need to take advanced math and the position paid more. Elan promptly filled out the required application for a transfer to the flight dispatcher department, which was mainly concerned with planning and operations control. At the same time, he confidently ordered the meteorology textbooks from the Department of Transportation.

He knew that the flight dispatch department was small and that the need for new trainees was rare. Yet, he kept a constant hope that he might be selected from among the many applicants.

Two years slowly passed. Elan had heard nothing from the flight dispatch department, but he kept studying weather and learning all the related operations control information. He knew that he was already two years older than the maximum age for initial consideration, yet he tenaciously believed it would all work out.

The phone call finally came from the flight dispatch office, asking Elan to come in for an interview. He was overjoyed at the news and, despite his age, he was selected. His transfer was effective almost immediately, and he enjoyed his career for the next twenty-five years until he retired. Elan says he believes that it was his "never-failing hope that eventually brought such fruitful results."

* * *

Beverly, a brown-eyed accountant from Detroit, turned up the volume on her determined hope for a shorter span of time, though no less meaningful or important. Lean and savvy, Beverly, a nineties kind of woman, had stayed single until she was almost thirty. She had many friends but no "significant other" until she was twenty-seven when she met and married Peter. After she first met Peter, he told her he had a four-year-old son. His ex-wife had acquired custody of the boy after an unpleasant marriage and a very nasty divorce. It wasn't long before Peter moved in with Beverly and his son Jason was visiting on the weekends.

The first time she met Jason, something about his sad, blue eyes reached deep inside Beverly. For some unexplain-

able reason, after Jason had fallen asleep, she wept uncontrollably. She and Peter were already very close and on several
occasions he cried, too. But he always knew why. He cried
because his ex-wife had custody of his son and he was
worried that she wasn't taking proper care of him.

Beverly, who says she has a strong spiritual belief, wasn't
worried; she was determined. Without hesitation, she told
Peter that they were good people, and, therefore, God would
show them the right way to get Jason back. One evening,
shortly after that declaration, Jason called Peter from his
mother's trailer. He was afraid because she had left him
alone and would not be home until late. Peter was not le-
gally allowed on his ex-wife's property, but that was no
problem for Beverly. Methodically and with great assurance, she called the police and asked them to meet her and
Peter at Jason's house. She then called Child Protective Services and later that same evening filled out a detailed report
with them.

When Jason's mom arrived home, she found a note saying that Jason was in protective custody. By the next
afternoon, Jason was living with Peter and Beverly, and custody petitions had begun. Peter's ex-wife never showed up
at the court hearing, and Peter and Beverly quickly gained
custody of Jason.

Even though Beverly longed from the first night she met
Jason that he would eventually live with them, she kept her
hope supply on high to counterbalance the reality of the
situation. She had seen many broken families go through
long court battles and pay enormous legal costs, but that
didn't stop her. She just hoped Jason would be theirs and, as
it turned out, she and Peter never even had to hire a lawyer.
Beverly believes it was her determined hope that helped all
this to happen.

That was almost seven years ago. Beverly now has a son
with Peter but she says that Jason will always be her first

baby. She never stopped to think that it wouldn't work out for her and Jason. She never doubted that adopting him wouldn't be best for her family. Her hope remained resolute.

* * *

In Utah, a homemaker named Brenda was applying her own brand of determined hope to her family's changing life style. They had recently begun a regular habit of tithing to their local church. That meant that each Friday, before paying any other bills, Brenda would write a check to the church for ten percent of her husband Seth's paycheck.

One particular week, however, after the tithing check was written and the rest of the bills were paid, they had $8.00 left in their checking account. The $8.00 was expected to cover the cost of food for a family of four as well as gas for Seth's weekly commute to work. Brenda would need to call on her own supply of hope to get through this one.

On their way to church that Sunday, they decided they just couldn't give that week and would hold onto the check until next week. However, once Brenda was in church and the offering had begun, she was overcome with hope that they had to give that check and that somehow it would be all right. She had no idea how, considering that $8.00 wouldn't go far toward feeding a family or fueling a truck. When she took the check from her purse, Seth nudged her arm with a reminding whisper, "I thought we were going to hang on to that!" Brenda had a strong sense that somehow God was working for their good. She responded that they just had to give it. Seth didn't argue.

She doesn't remember the sermon that day. Although she had just practiced the most determined kind of hope, she admits to mentally counting the beans left in the pantry and wondering how many ways she could cook them for her family. She says, "I knew that things would be fine in the long run, but I didn't think that God would just pour money into our pockets."

But that's exactly what He did! Within minutes after the sermon, a friend came up to Seth and asked about a bundle of chain-link fence Seth had had for sale. When Seth said, "Yes, it's still available," their friend said that he had a neighbor who needed it right away. If Seth took it to him that day, he could get paid for it when it was delivered. Within hours, Brenda and her family had received over twice as much money as they had given to their church, and "I didn't have to cook beans at all that week."

She has another story about determined hope that happened on the same day. Still basking in the hope found that morning, she suddenly remembered that the week before she had invited several families to their house that day for a potluck dinner. Each family was bringing its own meat, but, as hostess, Brenda had wanted to provide something extra. She asked Seth to pick up some vegetables on his way home from delivering the fence. He came home with only eight ears of corn. What was she to do with only eight ears when she knew more than eight people were coming to eat?

Brenda quickly split four ears for the children and cooked the remaining four ears whole. There were nine adults and six children, counting the members of her family. She was sure there wasn't enough for everyone. Yet, when the meal was finished, there was one whole ear of corn left over. Everyone insisted he or she had eaten corn and eaten plenty.

Brenda smiled to herself, remembering another time and place when something similar had occurred with some bread, some fishes, and a mass of hungry people. She is as determined in her hope today as she was a decade ago when she was blessed with enough food for her guests and enough funds for the week.

* * *

Determined hope has impeccable manners because it always answers an R.S.V.P. Julie, a mother-to-be from Albuquerque, got her R.S.V.P. from the determined side of hope early in her pregnancy.

She describes herself at that time as a happy expectant parent, yet she never really verbalized her situation as "I'm going to have a baby." Although she was indeed pregnant, somehow she did not "feel right" about it. In her case, determined hope would be emerging very soon.

Julie and her husband were on vacation at the Grand Canyon, a trip her doctor had approved. While standing on an overlook, viewing the silent massive sight, Julie started to hemorrhage. She was rushed to the closest medical facility and made it just in time to lie down on a scratchy blanket and deliver a baby girl—who would never take her first breath.

While the shock and sadness of loosing her baby was settling into her heart, she was quickly transferred to a local hospital where she just lay there wide awake, staring at the ceiling. Suddenly, the room was filled with a blazing light, brighter than any light she had ever seen. She became aware of the words, "Next time it will be all right." Although the words hadn't really been spoken, Julie heard them and she understood. She was determined that she would have another baby and that everything would work out just fine.

The words stayed in her mind for the next two years until she became pregnant again. This time, though her loved ones were worried, absolutely nothing could shake Julie's conviction that it would indeed be O.K. During this pregnancy, Julie went into premature labor, which frightened everyone in the family. But because of hope, she knew that she was not in danger and that the baby would be all right. She rested, and the labor pains stopped until the real birth occurred—six weeks later. Her son arrived quickly, easily, and was healthy.

Julie now uses those hopeful words in many other situations. "The first time something doesn't work out, I stop to see if I feel the promise of 'the next time.' If I do, I always know it will turn out O.K."

* * *

A couple in their seventies was on vacation when they, too, realized the power of determined hope. Avid outdoor people, Etta and her husband tapped into determined hope while on a camping trip in the wild with several other retired friends.

They were traveling to a campsite tucked in the backwoods of Oregon and had driven down a dirt road that was narrow and steep for the last ten miles. To get onto the road, they had to unlock a big metal gate, then lock it behind them. Etta usually enjoys the adventure of traveling from one camping spot to another, but she admits that she is "something of coward on that kind of road."

They finally found the campsite, and Etta went right to work at her job of leveling the trailer so the butane refrigerator would work. That is when she noticed a flat tire on one of the back dual wheels. Duals are huge, and she knew that none of the seniors they were traveling with could fix the tire. Yet, with determined hope for a quick solution, she quickly stood up, went into her trailer, and started to pray. When she returned outside, everyone asked her where she had gone. She confidently told them that she had gone inside to ask God to send her some help.

Within fifteen minutes, three strapping, young men came hiking through their camp. The event was unlikely, Etta explains, because no one else was supposed to be there—it was private property. Etta, however, was not afraid.

She knew they had come to help. Two of the men took turns at loosening the lugs, but it was the third man who finally succeeded. Together they quickly changed the tire and, just as suddenly as they came, they disappeared back into the woods.

The young men never mentioned why they were in that part of the woods, but Etta already knew. She never doubted for a minute that her prayer for help had been answered. She had packed the determined side of hope with all the rest of their camping supplies.

* * *

Because determined hope is predictable, you can plan, like Julie and the rest, how it can best benefit you. You can decide to invite it into your life and you can expect it to arrive. Think for a moment about an obstacle in your life or a fear you might have. How do you want to handle it? Do you feel determined about fixing your fear or outlasting your obstacle? Or do you feel like crumbling from the challenge?

There is no trick to enjoying the determined side of hope. Just say to yourself, "It will be okay, it will be okay, it will be okay." Keep saying that until you believe it, and when you open your eyes you will find yourself face to face with your own determined hope.

6

HOPE

IS EXHILARATING

*Enthusiasm is the yeast
that makes your hope rise to the stars."*

Walter Chrysler

Exhilarating hope is the easiest to recognize because, in most cases, it affects the body first. The personal accounts in this chapter describe a rush, a tingling, a twinge, or a heat sensation and "heart thumping" feelings. They describe feeling refreshed, relieved, and revived, and—whether their experience was many years ago or only moments ago—a belief that they have been forever changed. Exhilarating hope briefly brightens your view, heightens your senses, and leaves you with an energizing afterglow.

※ ※ ※

Virginia was only twenty-two when her son suffered what was later diagnosed as a seizure. When it happened, she was in a daze, a state of shock. She seemed to be watching herself and the events that followed from a detached, out-of-body place. She remembers that her son Tommy, who was nineteen months old at the time, had asked for a second glass of juice. Though he reached for it, his fingers never closed around the cup.

It all seemed to be in slow motion as he crumbled from a standing to a prone position on the floor with his eyes wide open. Before he reached the floor, Virginia's husband Martin asked him, "What is it? What do you see? Is there a bug on the floor?" By this time Virginia had said, "Take your cup." But when she saw his eyes staring at the floor, she too began looking at the floor to see what Tommy was staring at.

Slowly, he tried to bend his knees as Martin called his name. Tommy didn't answer. Then Martin said, "Something's wrong! He's having a seizure or something!" The panic Virginia felt at that moment was physical. She could still see everything happening but in the few moments after her husband said those words, "my awareness moved away from my physical body, through a black area, and then I became a complete observer—watching from a cool distance."

Because of her emotional distance, she was still safely detached when the ambulance arrived three minutes later. When Tommy's rigid little body was placed in the ambulance and she and Martin were in their car following him to the hospital, Virginia's feelings slowly shifted back to her physical body again—in a wonderful way.

She explains, "It was the first feelings of hope. It felt like bubbles building up in the area of my solar plexus. I began to actually feel the vibrating of every cell in my body. I felt as if I were having hot flashes alternating with shivers." The trauma had triggered her hope, and Virginia's body and thoughts became consumed with hope that Tommy would make it through this ordeal. She prayed to God for her son's well-being. She prayed that the emergency personnel would be skilled enough to help. Tommy's seizure lasted eleven minutes, and Virginia and Martin were able to bring him home from the hospital emergency room only forty-five minutes after they had arrived.

They had been so frightened, yet Virginia experienced exhilarating hope for the first time. She described feeling nourishment in every cell of her body, and her awareness was charged. She says she had a powerful feeling for the positive aspects of living. It was centered in her heart, yet she felt it from her hairline to her toenails. Virginia believes that her "hope was a lifeline to me so that I could get through a difficult situation."

While Virginia recalls that single visit from exhilarating hope, a young woman named Terry says she frequently feels physical rushes of hope. Most recently, she has been having a horrible time with finances. She's also supporting a young male friend named Kurt, who has fallen on hard times and can't seem to keep a job. Terry has offered him a place to stay. Luckily, exhilarating hope emerges and revives her just often enough to keep her spirits up.

Terry, like the rest of us, occasionally gets depressed and stressed about the lack of funds. Then she begins to build up resentment toward the person she is helping. She says that although Kurt keeps trying to get jobs, he finds only temporary ones and soon gets laid off. Recently though, he had gotten a job working at a fast-food restaurant and started to pay her back. But it is still very hard on Terry because she's worried that he will lose this job, too.

Terry holds down a full-time job plus two part-time ones while doing some free-lance work on the side. Normally she would have more than enough money for herself and Kurt. But, to make matters worse, she had taken in another roommate named Sue, to help with bills, then Sue suddenly lost her job. That makes three mouths to feed—Kurt's, Sue's, and hers.

Through it all Terry describes getting "bursts of hope from my heart center which would spread down to my stomach and up to my head. Really good ones would spread to my fingers and toes, and I would feel light-headed. I would be happy for twenty-four hours or longer (unless I went to the bank), and then I would revert to my usual pattern of worrying about money." She reviews these tingles from exhilarating hope: "The really 'vibrant' feelings of hope come during the worst of situations in my life. Yet, they keep on coming."

Terry is feeling exhilarating hope once again. She has been praying to find someone to help her with her taxes. "I always owe money." By "chance" she ran into a person who happened to be a good certified public accountant and for the first time in years she is getting money back in taxes. Terry says that, for her, when her life is full of worry, it's never long before her heart will be equally full of hope. Each problem triggers a spark of exhilarating hope to perk her up and strengthen her spirits.

* * *

Occasionally, hope is triggered by something visual—a picture or colors or lights—that sends hope surging through one's arms and legs. This is the kind of hope that one can see and feel. Following his parents' divorce, Shawn lived with his father in Sioux Falls, South Dakota. His father, a career air force officer, was then reassigned to a combat support unit in Southeast Asia. Shawn was only fifteen, yet he decided for himself to live with his aunt and uncle in another state rather than go back to his mother and siblings. This difficult decision had set the stage for the necessity of finding and feeling his own hope.

Though the move was traumatic for Shawn, the realization of his aloneness—even though he was in a warm and stable family—was even greater. On the day his father left for his overseas assignment, Shawn completely fell apart emotionally. He had no way of judging how long he cried—easily several hours. Then, "Suddenly, at the depth of my despair and from the darkness within my mind, a three-dimensional cluster of vibrant lights in the primary colors of the rainbow rose above me. The lights were alive."

A powerful voice spoke to him saying, "Fear not, for we are with you always." The presence stayed with him for a moment, and then slowly sank out of sight. Yet, a feeling of warmth remained with him the rest of the day as his despair eased. Though he still felt sorrow as he wept softly on and off for the rest of the day, he had felt the warmth of hope and seen its lights and colors.

Shawn adds that that brief, bright picture of hope helped him to cope and eventually to thrive in a new place, a new school, and a new home. It has provided him with hope and courage ever since. Now, many years later, he has decided that "It was a major step on this journey toward the Infinite for me."

❋   ❋   ❋

Another example of how hope comes in colors is told by Lynn. For almost two hours Lynn sobbed as she drove away from the man she believed was the love of her life. He no longer shared her feelings. She was miserable, desolate, and feeling so terribly alone and unloved that it was unbearable. Yet, as hopeless as Lynn felt about her life, she knew she had to stop crying in order to see the road.

She pulled off onto a ramp where she thought she had seen signs for a gas station, but there was no station—or anything else. Instead, in the middle of the day!, at the end of the ramp facing west, she stopped her car and gazed in disbelief at what she describes as "the most stupendous and awesome 'sunset' I have ever witnessed."

She had not seen so magnificent a one in all her forty-three years. She recalls, "It's hard to describe my feelings as I gazed at the glorious colors and the brilliance of the sky. Whenever I looked it was there. I sat quietly in my car. I had no thoughts, only incredible feelings of warmth and a oneness with the spectacular sight all around me. It gave me hope."

After some time Lynn's view paled, returned to daytime, and became normal again. But she kept the feeling of warmth and awe that had been triggered by that most unusual sunset. After what seemed like hours, which in reality had been only a short while, she regretfully started her car and began again to look for a gas station so that she could continue home. She had stopped crying for good.

Although this happened twenty years ago, it is an experience that she has never forgotten and is still vivid in her mind. She explains that she never shared this exhilarating episode with anyone until now because she feared others would laugh at her.

In her research project report she shared another episode—this one is also about tears, but this time they weren't hers. Lynn did eventually find the right man and married him. In February 1990, she, her husband Douglas, and their dog drove cross-country on vacation. When they stopped at El Paso, Texas, Lynn picked up several leaflets and brochures. One of them described the Weeping Madonna at a monastery in Blanco, Texas. Lynn felt deeply drawn to visit, but they were headed west and a northern detour was out of the question. As they continued west, her thoughts of a visit to the monastery kept recurring and she kept seeing more and more leaflets at all their different stopovers.

Their return trip to New York was to be a northern route but when they encountered snow in Flagstaff, Arizona, Douglas decided to take the southern route back home across the U.S.A. They drove south and once again ended up in El Paso, this time in a torrential blinding rainstorm. The following day, though the skies had cleared, Douglas decided he wanted to rest. To his consternation, Lynn left him and the dog and happily drove the two hours to Blanco all by herself.

The roads were fine until she pulled off the main road to drive up the mountain to the monastery. The narrow dirt road seemed to go nowhere. At one point, she stopped to ask the only person she saw, "an elderly man with a weather-beaten face and bright, clear blue eyes," if she were going in the right direction. His kindly face lit up and he said, "You're on the right path. People stop and often ask me. Soon they'll have to put up a sign."

Finally, Lynn reached her destination where a small group of Russian Orthodox priests lived and worked. There were several small white buildings sitting atop the mountain, against a beautiful, blue sky. A priest guided Lynn and one other tourist to the shrine that she had been so anxious to see. To Lynn's dismay, her fellow tourist, also from New York, talked incessantly. And much to her disappointment, the icon was not weeping when she saw it. There was, however, evidence of what could have been tear stains on the statue and a strong scent of myrrh. The priest blessed the statue and, after a brief, uneventful visit, they all left to tour the grounds.

They had been back in the church for some time while the priest was explaining the religious service, tradition, and history. Silently, Lynn was justifying to herself that, as a Catholic, a visit to any Russian Orthodox monastery was interesting and informative enough. So what if she didn't see the tears.

Suddenly, she became overwhelmed and surrounded by a very strong scent of myrrh. The priest assured her there was no myrrh in the church; he and Lynn's chatty companion did not smell anything. He continued with his discourse in the tiny, immaculate church and her talkative partner continued to give her weird glances. Lynn became oblivious to everything as her eyes searched the church for "something."

A sense of urgency demanded that she be excused from there to return to the altar of the Weeping Madonna. She went directly to the icon which stands behind a glass panel, and she was surprised to see what appeared to be teardrops at the bottom of the enclosure. Some of the drops were dried while others were actually sliding down the Madonna's dress. Lynn hesitantly reached around the glass and touched some of the tears. They were watery. Although the teardrops were disturbed by her touch, when she withdrew her hand they resumed their original position. Lynn tried to become logical and rational, and she searched the area to see if there was a leak dripping on the icon. She saw none. Though she tried to remain objective, she was tingling all over. The tears had triggered her hope.

She couldn't then—at age sixty—or now, several years later, fully understand the meaning of what she had seen. She went outdoors and found a young priest who hurried in to see what Lynn had witnessed. In those few seconds, most of the tears had dried, except that Lynn could see the dried spots which remained. The young priest was also unable to offer an explanation about the spots that had almost completely disappeared. He, too, searched for a possible water leak but found none on this clear, sunny day. Lynn was filled with bubbling, warm hope as she asked, "Why me?" The abbot could only say that at times the Mother of God may disclose a revelation to special individuals, but he could elaborate no further.

She went back outdoors and stood alone on the mountaintop. The sky above was a shimmering blue. The warm sun shone on everything as the sheep quietly grazed on the slope far below. Lynn describes her hopeful feelings: "I felt incredibly at peace and as if I were humming with everything. I felt warm and safe as though there were nothing between me and heaven above." Her return trip to the motel was a happy one. She was full of hope and pride at the idea that the Mother of God had singled her out.

Unlike her beautiful daytime sunset of twenty years ago that she had kept secret, Lynn tried to share this experience with her husband, but he debunked it completely. He said it was just another money-making scheme. For a while his attitude put a damper on her mood, but then she remembered her feelings when she touched those heavenly tears and the hope that tingled throughout her body. That wondrous experience is still clearly etched in her mind and in her being. She's convinced that "No one and nothing can alter that."

✳ ✳ ✳

High hopes emerged in Valery during Christmas, the time of year when emotions are often most fragile. If you're already happy at Christmas, the season can make you giddy. But if you're emotionally struggling when Christmas arrives, the season can send you downward into a state of self-pity.

In July of that year Valery had been fired from her job as an administrative assistant. After several months of soul searching, she decided to use this opportunity to make the most of her skills. In an effort to utilize all of her professional talents in an environment that was conducive to her soul growth, she decided to start her own résumé and career consulting service for other displaced workers.

With the new company, however, Valery had difficulty making enough money to support herself, especially in light of a declining economy. By Christmas, she was very disheartened because she couldn't even afford to buy Christmas presents for her family and friends. She didn't know where the next month's rent money would come from. Feeling all alone, in the midst of the merriest season of the year, Valery prayed for the strength to carry on and for some direction toward what she calls "achieving solvency."

A friend invited her to another friend's house for Christmas. The hostess, Sherri, whom Valery had never met, was so open and warm to her that it lifted her spirits instantly. Sherri sensed that Valery was in dire straits, so she played a motivational tape that helped immensely. As they said good night, Sherri hugged her and told her to remember that through faith in God there is always hope.

None of this advice struck Valery as "new," yet she marveled that this stranger seemed to know that she needed support and encouragement and also knew just what to say and do. The evening really helped Valery because it triggered her own supply of exhilarating hope. When she left the party, her body was tingling with anticipation.

The next morning, she received a flood of phone calls from close friends and family, as well as from people whom she hadn't heard from in years. She says, "It was almost uncanny that everyone told me that I was a very special person, recounting events in which I had inspired them or reminding me of times when I had achieved something difficult."

All of the callers told her about a unique situation in

which she had changed their life for the better. She would no sooner hang up the phone with one person than another would call to provide the same message. She says she felt like George Bailey, the character played by Jimmy Stewart in the movie *It's a Wonderful Life*. Valery had such an opening of her heart center, remembering in a very personal way that no one is poor when one has friends.

She knows that the advice from Sherri and the phone calls the next day were the answers to her prayers. "I felt a sense of confidence and an electric surge of hope pulsing through my body. When the holidays were over, I went back to work with a new energy, knowing that God would provide for me even when things seem completely desolate." She concludes, "I am still struggling financially, but each month I seem to have just enough to get by. My hope carries me."

* * *

Not as dramatic as Valery's exhilarating hope but certainly as significant is the story from Mel. Mel offers an experience with hope that happened when he was in a deep depression. He had just gone into "early retirement." What that really means, he explains, "is that the architectural business was so bad that I needed the Social Security payment just to pay the rent on my apartment."

At sixty-two, he was beginning to feel that life had no purpose and that he might as well end it all. After some days of real agony, Mel started looking through a book which described what he was feeling as the "obscure night." Slowly, some change started to come over him and he began to feel a lifting of this burden. He started feeling better.

This change was not immediate. His was a more subtle feeling of hope, a softer version of the other stories, "more of a feeling of slowly walking into the light from a very dismal place. I could see the brightness and feel the warmth."

Since that feeling of hope, Mel says he has "chosen to ride out life and just take whatever comes." His attitude has become, "If I took my own life, I would not be able to help others because of my experience. If the Universe steps in and snuffs out my life, that is O.K., too."

* * *

Like Mel, Kathy considered ending it all. She took it one step further, however, and actually tried to end her life just before hope stirred inside her and changed her mind. At thirty-nine, Kathy was still recovering from her divorce. She was alone except for two dogs. She had been in two relationships in the three years following her divorce that had left her feeling more lonely and with less self-esteem. Her job was depressing and she felt worthless. She lived in an area of town with little to offer except bars.

At first, she had stayed in West Virginia, because of her parents. But her father had died eight years ago, and her mother had recently returned to Pennsylvania because she needed special medical care that was not available locally. Although Kathy's job was killing her ambition and enthusiasm, she had contributed more than ten years to a pension and was afraid to start over at her age.

On the night of her most recent boyfriend's birthday, she went to a bar and nearly drank herself to death. Failing that, she attempted to drive home. She still has great pain thinking about what happened next because after three years she can remember it all too well. She rounded a curve and slid into a telephone pole. Her head struck the windshield, but she did not fly through it because, by some miracle, she had fastened her seat belt. Kathy survived, but her car was destroyed. All she could say over and over was, "How could I be so stupid!" During the next week, she ate very little and took a combination of pain pills and nerve pills.

One morning she awakened to chirping birds. The sound seemed very loud, almost as if they were barking. The strange sounds started Kathy thinking about how close she had come to never hearing those sounds again. "I felt awake all over, not just my ears. I started to tingle all over and my body was stretching and yawning and fighting the effects of my painkillers." She shook her head to clear her thoughts, and suddenly she knew she had to pull herself together and make some changes in her life. Now feeling the physical effects of exhilarating hope instead of depression, she decided she would find a purpose for living.

Since that morning when the birds magnified their songs for Kathy and woke up her own hope, she has met a wonderful man whose family has accepted her into their family. She changed jobs and is now teaching first grade. She has the gift of knowing that she has made a difference in some of the children's lives. And she is hopeful that her giving to others will show how grateful she is to have been given a second chance.

Some of her emotional scars are not completely healed, but "I continue to have a great deal of hope for the future— in both my personal and professional life." Her exhilarating hope woke her from a depressing, drug-covered mood and convinced her to try again, promising more tingles in the future.

❋ ❋ ❋

Ella, a young mother of four, received her bolster of hope not from the birds, but from another young mother. When recalling her story, she considers the old adage, "When God wants to give you a message, he asks a human to deliver it." The message this time was to recognize her own exhilarating hope.

Besides caring for her seven-year-old, five-year-old twins, and a nine-month-old baby, Ella is active as a volunteer leader in LaLeche League. The League is a support organization for mothers who want to breast-feed their babies. Ella runs a group meeting and also does telephone counseling and home visits with mothers who are having difficulties breast-feeding.

Recently several of the mothers she counseled had weaned their babies too soon, despite the fact that she had spent many of her own hours helping them and reassuring them. One woman even weaned her newborn because the doctor told her that her baby was "allergic to breast milk." Ella felt that that was a medical impossibility but could do nothing to convince the new mom that her own milk was better for her baby.

She was feeling so hopeless after these events that she even considered quitting her work with the LaLeche League. She thought perhaps she was no longer effective in helping these mothers and that someone else might do a better job. To lift her spirits, she began reading inspirational literature, including a book called *The Edgar Cayce Primer* by Herbert B. Puryear, Ph.D. Although her reading was helpful, she still considered quitting the League.

One day she went shopping with her youngest child and saw a woman who was very pregnant buying bottles and sterilizing equipment. Ella thought to herself, "I wonder if she has even considered breast-feeding?" She toyed with the idea of bringing up the subject, but didn't need another rejection so she said nothing. She remembers thinking to herself, "It is her responsibility. If she wants to know about breast-feeding, she can just ask someone."

As she got ready to leave the store, Ella felt a tap on her shoulder. It was the pregnant woman!

"Excuse me," she said, "Do you breast-feed your baby?"

"Yes," Ella said in shock.

"Do you like it? Could you tell me what I have to do to breast-feed my baby?"

Ella gave her all the information she needed, as well as her phone number in case she had any problems.

As she went to her car, she felt the tingling signs of hope—hope because she was convinced about continuing her work with the League and hope for another new mom she had just helped by sharing her knowledge and offering her support. Ella says, "I was so excited. I knew I had been given a signal from God to continue on with my work. I knew that I was doing important work. I felt energized and alive."

* * *

Sandy felt his own exhilarating hope in the early eighties while, at age thirty-five, he was looking back and reviewing one of his life's major choices. He recalled that his hope had "given me a new feeling for the positive side of life."

About twenty years earlier, Sandy had traveled from his Canadian homeland to England and had become involved in what he considered a "permanent situation." He easily settled into a new life style and was profoundly happy with his work and surroundings. In due course, he says, "I became emotionally attached to a wonderful girl." They planned to marry and, at that point in his life, Sandy felt he was in complete harmony with everything and everyone around him. He was happy with his choices and excited about the prospects of what his future years in England would hold.

Suddenly he was unexpectedly recalled to Canada on very short notice. Once back home he realized he might be unable to return to England on a permanent basis. "The girl whom I planned to build a life with was patient and waited for a long time, but when it became totally obvious that I could not return, she took another path and we lost contact."

At that point Sandy became very bitter. All that was good and positive seemed to have been taken away, and he was left with a situation over which he had no control. For many years he remained bitter and resentful and could find nothing that would reflect a positive side to his life. In time he married someone else and helped raise two beautiful children. He says that, through it all, he has been blessed "in the material sense with a comfortable life." He is grateful to have been able to provide well for his family.

Until a few years ago, however, his thoughts would still drift back to England and he would, on many occasions, ask himself all of the "what if's." "It was about that time that I became interested in the A.R.E. and the Edgar Cayce readings. Through the Cayce material, I was able to understand my relationship to God and my environment. I began to realize that there is a purpose to life. I let go of my feelings of resentment about abandoning my life's plan in England because I came to understand that there is a reason for it all." He says that his new hopeful attitude energizes his current feelings of contentment and that he feels lighter and happier than he has for years.

Sandy explains, "I have come to accept and understand that there was a reason that I was directed onto my current path. The other path, the one that led me to England, is perhaps for another time. I have come to be content with that thought. There is a warm peaceful hope from letting go of the past."

✳ ✳ ✳

There are extremes with the exhilarating side of hope—feelings ranging from invigoration to a warm, fuzzy contentment. Your own experience of hope can be triggered by a scene like Lynn's sunset or a feeling like Virginia's reassuring tingles of courage. It might just be a new enthusiasm about the life you have, like Sandy feels. No matter how it touches you, you'll recognize it every time. It's so clear and so joyous that you'll just have to pause and welcome your hope with gusto.

7
HOPE
IS FLEETING

"...with an atom
of hope, then, little by little
comes awakening to the possibilities."

Based on Edgar Cayce Reading 5749-11

There is a kind of hope that is swift and nimble—here one moment and gone the next. Fleeting hope is sure and agile and can easily go unnoticed; still, it manifests in those quiet, quick reminders that we do indeed have cause to hope. There will be no great visions or bolts of light to signal the fleeting side of hope, so look carefully. Speak softly in its presence and don't reach out to hold it hard for it will disappear in your hands. Instead, honor it for what it gives you—a pause in your pain and a new point of view.

* * *

Art was dying—or so the medical professionals said. They had predicted that in six more months he would be gone. Throughout his illness, he and his wife Bonnie maintained an intense belief that he would be cured. Up to his last stay in the hospital, he dreamed of the day when he would be cured and could travel across the country in a motor home and speak of his miracle cure to packed audiences.

But that is not the way it happened. Art died in 1988. He left behind his widow, Bonnie, who was without a husband and now without hope. Bonnie hated the term "widow." She wrote it over and over again on pieces of paper all over the house as if to convince herself that the term had really become her life's label. One day, quite by accident, she misspelled the dreaded word and accidentally inserted the letter "n" into it, coming up with the word "window." Unbeknownst to her at the time of the "mistake," she had literally breathed a breath of hope into the hated word.

When she read her new word, she actually enjoyed the thought of being a "window" and imagined herself bringing light into her own life. She had no way of knowing then that the act of adding an insignificant letter to a word she knew by heart would give her hope for the future. Because she noticed the new word, her whole life changed and she went on to become a source of hope for other widows and widowers. She continues to guide them along their way. With her new label, she has been slowly able to face her many trials. When she was lonely or afraid, she just kept thinking of herself as a "window" and that kept her feeling hopeful. In time, Bonnie began teaching classes, forming support groups, and sharing information with the hundreds of people she had met along the way.

Today, from a healthy, time-healed place, Bonnie looks back to a period before her new life began. She says, "The words 'to live again' meant nothing to me at the dawn of the new year of 1988. Art and I had spent Christmas in our beautiful rental condo. We had been going down every weekend to revamp, clean, and paint so that it would be spotless for rental in January.

"Art had just taken a physical exam, but we didn't yet know the results. He seemed to tire easily as he weeded the small garden outside our patio door. For some months, it seemed as if he were taking an increased number of noon-time naps, but he always liked to 'catch forty winks' after lunch, so I thought nothing of it." They would not get the results of those tests until the middle of January. On January 21, he left for the doctor's office only to return home and tell Bonnie that the doctor was called out on an emergency. In truth, he was so shocked about being told he had pancreatic cancer that he couldn't tell his wife. He couldn't even face the truth himself, so how could he tell Bonnie that he only had six months to live?

When Bonnie got to work, she decided to call the doctor herself. She was told that they had been trying to reach her, so she left work immediately and went to the doctor's office, where he explained in detail all the facts. Now Bonnie was filled with shock and disbelief. Slowly she drove home to talk to Art and to make plans for what they could do to help him find a cure. She was convinced that she would not be a widow in six months or anytime, ever. No matter how they tried—even working with a nutritionist and attending a well-known cancer clinic in Mexico—there was no change. The cancer had spread too far and was already established in the intestines.

Day after day the grueling treatments took their toll on Art's strength, until one day while sitting on the patio enjoying the warm sun, he fell. He was so weak that Bonnie wondered how she could get him down the outside stairs and into the car. As she was desperately struggling, the doorbell rang. It was their friend who said, "I have no idea why I'm here, but something told me to come!" The friend helped Bonnie get Art to the car, and Bonnie drove him to the emergency room. "Within a week he had slipped away. It was at 5:00 a.m. Dawn of a new day. A new beginning for Art. A new path and a new life."

Now, Bonnie has a new life, too. She has her classes, her students, and all the joy of helping other people to cope with the death of a spouse. Her first day of hope was when she noticed the importance of her misspelled word. The incident was a fleeting one and could have easily gone unnoticed, but because a letter "accidentally" landed on her piece of paper, Bonnie is indeed a "window" through which others, in their grief and sadness, can begin to see a happier life.

* * *

When Rebecca's husband became sick with bipolar illness, her hope was awakened by a creature of nature. Neither glamorous nor exotic, her hope came with the unusual and fleeting opportunity of seeing a turkey in the wild.

The disease that gripped Rebecca's husband had thrown him into a deep depression that led him to leave their relationship and, for that matter, all his relationships. He ran away to isolate himself. She was concerned for months, but trusted in God. When she got to a very low point of despair and was not sure whether she should continue to hope for health and healing or to move on with her life, she asked God for a sign.

Rebecca had always loved the very rare appearance of wild turkeys in the countryside of rural Connecticut near where she lived. So "I went for a drive and I asked to see a turkey. I told myself that if I saw a turkey I would remain hopeful." In less than a mile, she had to literally stop her car because a flock of turkeys was squawking and scooting across the road. The sight of them triggered her hope.

Her husband did return and things gradually improved. Then, two years later, because of the same emotional problems and illness, he again went into sudden isolation and Rebecca was again wondering if she dared ask for the "turkey" sign. A second sighting would require a keen eye and expert timing. She decided to go for a drive. In less than five minutes, she stopped her car in shock. In the distance she saw the rare sight of a group of turkeys in a large field engaged in a mating ritual. She felt this was a blessing and again "my sign to have hope for healing our relationship, perhaps a quick remission for my husband, or even a total recovery." She concluded hopefully, "We'll see."

For Bonnie it was a single letter, for Rebecca it was a glimpse of one of God's creatures. What can it be for you? Think about something small and fleeting that usually goes unnoticed yet could make you feel hope. What are the little symbols of hope that could bring you peace of mind and happiness? In the next story, a woman found hope in the words to a song.

✳ ✳ ✳

Nancy discovered hope in 1978. She had reached the depths of despair, unable to function at home and unable to work. Now she was suicidal. Her depression had been serious for the past fifteen years and she had tried shock treatments, drugs, and five different psychiatrists but only got worse. Then one night she could not sleep, so she played "I Want to Live," a John Denver song that moved her deeply. The words to the song were: "I want to live. I want to grow. I want to see. I want to know. I want to share what I can give. I want to be. I want to live." (Copyright © 1977 Cherry Lane Music Co., ASCAP) Out of a whole album, those few stanzas could have easily gone unnoticed. But, for Nancy, these simple words triggered her hope.

Nancy played the record over and over all night long. In the morning she knew what she had to do. Her instincts led her to the church of her childhood, where she realized that she had much to do to change her life. She suddenly knew that she had to move out of her mother's house and into an apartment of her own. She also realized that she had to find a way to bring her friends back into her life.

With her new hope, Nancy found the energy to move in the next month, and soon her friends were visiting her again. Those simple lyrics could have easily gone in one ear and out the other, but instead they had struck a note in her heart. A fleeting stanza of music had changed her life. She is still amazed at how remarkable her turnaround was. "Previously, I had been bedridden by my depression. But I got up and did what I knew God wanted me to do."

Another woman, named Claire, was also in need of a new existence and new hope. Her present life was not going the way she had planned. Then one day she recognized her own powers of hope. For only an instant and for only her eyes, fleeting hope paused long enough to remind her that hope is always there, you just have to recognize it.

Claire was sitting by the edge of a peaceful river in Oregon. It was early summer and the sun was rising. The rest of her family was hiking farther ahead around the bend and she was completely alone. Suddenly the thought came very strongly into her mind that deer come to this spot in the morning to drink. Luckily, Claire had her camera with her.

She sat there for some time, holding her camera ready, but nothing happened. Finally, she set it down next to her and gazed at the ground, lost in her own thoughts. When she looked up again, she saw two beautiful golden does shining in the morning light. They were crossing the river to investigate the quiet, thoughtful human who was sitting at their watering spot.

"My mind was thrilled and I was filled with the most fantastic hope." She knew that if she reached to get her camera, they would run, but she just had to have a picture. She reached and the deer bolted, but not before she snapped her camera several times. Out of the photos that she took, only one turned out—a picture of one doe still in the water and the other leaping into the bushes. "I had it enlarged and still look at it to prove to myself that lovely things can and do happen every once in a while."

For Claire, no applause accompanied her hope, no lightning, no thunder, no bright beams of light. Just a glimpse of a pair of nature's fleeting creatures to remind her that although her life right now was not what she had planned, her future would be filled with lovely things. Edgar Cayce once said, "For in nature and in the animal instincts we find only the expressions of a universal consciousness of hope, and never of fear . . . " (2067-1) Claire and Rebecca would completely agree.

✳ ✳ ✳

It was many years ago when Evelyn first recognized her own signs of hope. She is no longer sure what dilemma was consuming her at the time, but she does recall that she was pondering an important decision and had been feeling very down for days trying to make it.

Finally she made up her mind one evening while she was doing dishes, but then decided that she needed a second opinion. She said to God, "If this is right, You'll have to let me know." Suddenly a soft, fragile breeze blew in the window; that confirmed her choice. Evelyn knew that God had sent that answer because there had been no breeze before and the air was still the rest of the day.

Evelyn adds, "For me hope comes through nature. If I'm down, it's those magic moments like sunshine on a cloudy day or blue jays at the feeder. For me the subtle reminders from nature give me hope."

* * *

Jeff and Sylvia found their own hope through nature, too. From a tree—a very special tree. Like most young couples, when they were first married, they had no money. Jeff was out of work and things "in general were haywire." It was Christmas and, for both of them, a deeply spiritual time of year. They were depressed driving home from their search for a Christmas tree because they couldn't even afford $10 to buy one. It was their first Christmas and they had wanted it to be special.

As they turned up the country road which led to their small rented cottage, the night felt so oppressive that it only amplified their sadness and resignation. In the distance, the car headlights picked up an object in the middle of the road. They could only tell from that distance that the object was quite large.

As they came closer, a sense of peace and hope came over them. They approached the object and stopped their car, both stunned with elation. There, in the middle of the dark deserted road, already cut, lay the most perfect Christmas tree they had ever seen and—Jeff adds—"have ever seen since. It was indeed a very special Christmas." Jeff and Sylvia have had many Christmases since, but none as memorable as the night they found a tree serendipitously in the middle of nowhere on a snowy, lonely road. For them, finding their perfect Christmas tree triggered their hope.

There are so many little events that trigger hope. A tiny

tender breeze, a pair of does in the woods, and even a tiny letter written incorrectly on a page. Look a little closer for the unnoticed signs of hope around you that can change your life forever—or at least for the holidays, like for Jeff and Sylvia.

* * *

Nearly a decade ago, Jacqueline found herself becoming extremely depressed. She was in an emotionally stressful work place inhabited by what she calls "noncohesive personnel." She and her husband had never been truly suited for one another, and he was not supportive of their marriage nor concerned about her stressful work situation.

To compound the matter, their daughter Amy was going through a lot of problems, trying to support her own two children while obtaining a college degree following a divorce from her drug-addicted husband. At the other end of the family tree, her mother had begun to deteriorate mentally, a condition later diagnosed as Alzheimer's disease. Jacqueline's church was of little help at the time; it was going through a split in philosophy. In her search for help, she was led to a membership in the A.R.E.

A short time later, on a clear, sunny day, her husband came into the house, grabbed her elbow, and urged her outside, saying, "I think you should see this." He pointed up to a single cloud in an otherwise cloudless sky. The lone cloud was hanging low in front of their house. Jacqueline felt she could almost reach up and touch it. It had shaped itself into the outline of a heart. The center was hollow.

She ran for her camera and got a picture of it just as the cloud was starting to break up. More important than the photo, though, was that she knew intuitively that this was a fleeting sign of hope and spiritual love. To her, it meant that she could literally "take heart" and feel hope. In recalling the story, she says, "My husband does not usually take stock in symbolic meanings or personal reflection, but even he was impressed."

Since then, not only has her marriage improved, but they have also found a wonderful caregiver for her mother. Their daughter, now graduated from college, has found a great job. Amy's ex-husband went into rehabilitation and seems to be getting his life back on track.

Now, many years later, Jacqueline has retired from her job, and she and her husband have moved to a beautiful, peaceful home by the Pacific Ocean. "Here, I am finding and resolving my own inner conflicts through meditation, researching, and writing." She is surrounded daily by nature's messages of hope, but none are as important as the puffy, fleeting heart-shaped cloud that she saw during a very cloudy time in her life.

* * *

Although Cameron was raised in a warm, typically suburban family and was blessed in many ways, he was often a sad, shy, and lonely child. Even today, in his adult life, he finds it easy to slip into feelings of despair.

When growing up, he had to consciously work at and search for a better outlook on life. He has found his brighter outlook bit by bit in books and prayers and through observation. He refers to the inspiration from the Edgar Cayce readings and other sources as the building blocks of his hope. In full mental consciousness he now knows that there is light ahead. He has hope.

Yet, as a young child, "I did not have this ability to summon hope into my stressful situations. Prayers, to a young child waiting for an immediate response, seemed a waste of time."

In retrospect, however, he recalls that hope did find its

way to him. "It came to me in unexpected smiles and the tone of voice with which someone greeted me, the sight of a baby rabbit, or the first warm days of spring. We live in a fast and physical world; perhaps, when I was a child, the greater truth had shown through in these subtle, small sparks of God's beauty. Though they may seem to be insignificant, they were the moments I held onto and they gave me hope."

* * *

Hope came early in Larry's life, too. As a youth of sixteen, he was going through a very difficult time. His parents had reared him very strictly and, therefore, left him little leeway to express his emotions or to release his anger. Consequently, he had a lot of feelings bottled up inside. He felt little satisfaction in his life or in any aspect of living. The previous year, his mother had died of cancer after many years of fighting her pain and illness. Understandably, Larry felt great emptiness, loneliness, and frustration.

During this frustration and emptiness, his sister came to him one evening just before bedtime and said, "I think you'd like to read this." It was a small book entitled *Prayer Works* by an Episcopal bishop named Austin Pardue. The book is about recognizing one's spiritual nature and how to use it.

As Larry began reading it, he kept saying to himself, "This is just what I need." The more he read, the more he discovered. "I felt as if I had another limb, even a whole body that I'd been ignoring all these years. I felt like a horse put out to green pastures or a starving man unexpectedly sitting down to a feast." Larry was feeling his own hope because of the simple kindness of his sister's gift. The gesture could have gone unnoticed or, worse, the book could have gone unread. But luckily Larry opened the book and, thanks to his sister, found his own hope.

He read one brief chapter each night, meditated on it,

and went to sleep. "I became immersed in an ocean of energy and consciousness, which healed my life of tawdry concerns. I have never been the same since."

* * *

The signs of hope are sometimes small. They can be triggered by a simple gesture like giving someone a book, noticing a cloud, or feeling a breeze. Sometimes the common everyday, explainable incidents don't seem to have much significance on the surface. But, for those people who recognize the symbols, fleeting hope has completely changed their lives.

If you're feeling hopeless, try looking up at the sky or walking in the woods or driving a new and different way home from work. Stop at the store and buy a fresh flower, plant some seeds in a window-sill planter, or call up an old friend to say "Hi." Look carefully for hope; keep a keen eye out for little, natural miracles.

8
HOPE
IS HEALING

*"He who has health
has hope. He who has
hope has everything."*

Arabian Proverb

Hope can actually help to make and keep us well.
With a hopeful attitude we can be more physically fit and we can stay in a sound condition to
better face the challenges of our lives. Healing
hope is an over-the-counter remedy. You don't need anyone to write you a prescription; you just need to reach inside
yourself for your own dosage.

* * *

Vira was in her fifties when she first discovered her internal supply of healthy hope. At the time, she was experiencing pain on her right side to the extent that, when riding

in the car, she had to lift her right side because each bump on the road increased the pain. She went to the doctor, and he diagnosed an ovarian cyst. Because of Vira's age, the doctor recommended a complete hysterectomy and set the date for the operation for three weeks.

On the way home, she stopped at the drugstore to pick up a book to read so she wouldn't have to think about her pending operation. As she stood scanning the rack of reading material, she spotted a magazine with a bold headline highlighting an article on ovarian cysts. She bought it and returned home.

The article was very depressing; it stated that most ovarian cysts are malignant. After reading it, Vira flipped through the magazine and read another article on how visualization was being used on cancer patients. It mentioned that in some cases visualization reduced the size of tumors or eliminated them altogether.

"This article gave me hope," she says. "For two weeks, each time I took my iron supplement capsule, I envisioned a new army of white corpuscles with swords joining my regular army—stabbing the cyst over and over again." In two weeks the cyst burst, and a painful trip to the hospital confirmed that the cyst was gone and had passed through her menstrual tract. No operation was needed.

It seems that Vira's "army" had done its job. Her hopeful visualization, as a result of a magazine headline, had helped her to mobilize her own defense system and avoid an intrusive operation.

※　※　※

Gerard, like Vira, used visualization in a remarkable self-cure. While working on an electrical circuit of 220 volts, he received third-degree burns on his right hand. "It charred my skin so badly it was crisp and literally pushed forward on my fingers in little ripples of hard, burned skin."

The doctor's suggestion was to submerge the hand in cold water to help him tolerate the pain and to come in the next day to do some possible skin grafting. The soaking helped, but in those quiet moments of holding his hand in the icy water, Gerard says that he remembered stories of healing he had read in the Edgar Cayce material and in other literature as well.

Instead of returning to the doctor the next day, he visualized his hand healing itself. He concentrated on a brilliant shaft of light penetrating his flesh and exuding healing energy. "No other effort was expended on my part," he explains, "except conscious realization and remaining in a state of meditation and hopefulness." He didn't use bandages or salves, just summoned his own hope to heal his hand.

On the fourth day following the accident, Gerard walked into the doctor's office to show him his hand. It was completely healed except for a slight tenderness of the flesh underneath. No scars or discoloration was visible. The doctor's only reaction was to examine Gerard's hand carefully and say, "Hmmm. I have no explanation for this other than it is a miracle."

* * *

Many years ago, Bertha learned that a cataract in her right eye was threatening to close off her vision completely. As she was driving home down a narrow road, the thought of the cataract was filling her with sadness and fear. She had been told by her ophthalmologist that an operation was not advisable due to the danger of traumatizing the still-good left eye. She was also wondering that "with my youngsters still of school age, I was in very tight financial circumstances—what could I do with only one good eye?"

As she slowed to a stop at an intersection, a large luxury

convertible stopped beside her. The tanned and sun-glassed driver asked her if she could tell him the way to the Triple R Ranch. "You're O.K.," she replied. "Just go on up about two miles. It's on the left." He thanked her and then, just as he put his car in gear, added, "Do you know that you have very beautiful eyes?" He drew out the plural, so that it sounded like "eyezzzz." While she sat stunned for the moment, he pulled away quickly, without saying another word.

Bertha drove on slowly, feeling that he must have sensed her need. She felt that his message was a gift of encouragement and hope. She never did have the operation, and the vision in her right eye remained a dark, cloudy veil against her world. Yet, remaining hopeful through the following years, she recalled that beautiful experience a thousand times and says, "I'll bless that man forever!"

Later, Bertha went on to become a vision and eye coordination therapist, helping others who suffer from all kinds of vision problems. Nearly a quarter of a century later, she received a small gift of gratitude from a woman whose son had benefited from this type of therapy under Bertha's tutelage.

The gift was a tiny bottle of aloe vera eye drops, something she had never heard of before. "Using it twice daily, to my amazement and great joy," she explained, "I began to see light through the inner corner of my right eye—within about two weeks. Encouraged, I applied the drops (to both eyes) three to four times daily from then on, and little by little as the weeks and months passed, the lens cleared." At last all that remains of the cataract substance is a pin-dot-size bit occasionally referred to as a "floater."

"For over twenty years," she adds, "I had been offering vision therapy as well as other treatments to many of the kids who entered my private, remedial education program. During the healing of my right eye, I found it necessary to perform, for myself, a number of the corrective exercises I'd been teaching the kids for all those years! Since the muscles of my right eye had virtually ceased to function, it took some time to regain binocularity. In truth, the whole process was rather fun! And I shared it all with my students who took a keen interest."

Bertha continues, "During the healing of my right eye (and since), my eye doctor increased my intake of vitamins C, A, E, and zinc in order to prevent, if possible, any future cataract. I'm now almost seventy-five, and so far, all's well. Of course," she adds, "my diet is loaded with fresh veggies and salads."

Bertha's story of healthy hope shows the importance of using and sharing our own reservoir of wellness. Her account personifies the old adage of what goes around comes around. When she was deeply worried and distressed about the potential loss of vision in her eye, some stranger came along in a car and awakened her hope. She went on to spend the next two decades giving other people hope by helping them to better see the world around them. Finally she received a gift of natural healing drops of aloe vera—for her eyes only. With hope in her heart, she applied the drops. Now she is as healthy as the people for whom she has cared.

* * *

Ray was able to write his own prescription for a medical problem that was affecting his work and his freedom of choice. After receiving his master's degree in education, he began teaching English in a senior high school in New Jersey. He realized that he felt very sick whenever he entered the building. So he researched and discovered that the building had its own recycling air system and windows which couldn't be opened. Thus, the building had no fresh air. He was so uncomfortable that he had to resign after the first semester.

Four years later, he was offered a teaching assignment that he really wanted, but it meant going back into the same building! Ray prayed for guidance and received his answer in a dream. He saw himself carrying a silver bowl. The bowl was filled with what he calls a golden "goop," which he understood to be a mixture of butter, sesame seeds, and raw garlic. He woke up full of hope that this remedy would allow him to work at a job that he really wanted.

Ray bought the ingredients the next day and mixed up his "first super-butter goop." He then telephoned the principal and accepted the job. "I ate a quarter to half a teaspoon every day while I worked at that high school," Ray says, "and my health was much better. I was able to tolerate the building so then I could do the work I loved."

Tara started paying attention to her health about eight years ago, but it took some time and effort to finally figure out what was wrong. At age fifty-three, she had difficulty with her arm getting stuck in various positions, and different parts of her body would ache with an intensity that was hard to tolerate. Since she was already familiar with some methods of self-healing and prayer, she put off going to a doctor, hoping she could cure herself. "An inner voice kept telling me to go to a doctor but," she says, "I was not listening."

In the meantime, her mother had a stroke, and Tara began taking care of her. She also broke her wrist while lifting her mother and wore a cast for six weeks. Like most of us, Tara was too busy taking care of other people instead of sorting out her own feelings about her self and her health. After the cast was removed, she did not take the time for therapy because of her mother's need for constant care. Her wrist was better, but she still had to keep her arm in an upright position. Through it all, her daughter insisted that Tara needed physical therapy. She admits that at that point "I was getting concerned because I was dropping things with my right hand. But my mother took all my time, and I couldn't or wouldn't take the time to find out what was wrong with me."

After three years, Tara finally had to place her mother in a nursing home. Then she began to take a serious look at herself. Her whole right side was affected now and she wasn't able to make the simplest movements, like waving or clapping her hands. Then one morning she woke up and couldn't see out of her right eye. She made all kinds of excuses for this but knew she was only kidding herself. That night she asked for a sign as to what to do. It seems she was finally ready to look at her own life and to try to make it better.

The next morning, Tara accidentally sat on her glasses and broke them. Then she knew it was time for a doctor. Since her eye was of paramount concern, she went to her eye doctor. He checked her thoroughly and said he couldn't do anything for her, that she should see a neurologist because he thought it could be multiple sclerosis (MS).

Tara went to a neurologist who treated her "like a neurotic woman who was suffering from empty-nest syndrome." He did, however, order tests to discern if it was MS. The tests showed no MS, and he dismissed Tara, saying she should see an ophthalmologist. She did as he suggested; he found nothing wrong with her eye, but said that he thought she had MS. She was back to square one.

During all this time, Tara feels that she was experiencing many small healings. Her acute pains were disappearing, her eye cleared up to where she only had double vision, and her arm didn't get stuck any more. She still had tremendous weakness, however. Her hand and foot had begun to shake. She became very discouraged and frustrated with the medical profession and decided she was through with them. She would do it on her own. "Of course," she says, "I just kept getting worse." The little steps of progress were hopeful, but other symptoms kept appearing. She was confused about what to do next.

The spiritual group she was attending at the time used guided visualization as part of their program. One night the visualization included seeing and asking Jesus a question. So Tara asked Jesus about her health. She was told that she would be healed eventually, but that she should use this time to learn compassion and caring for others weaker in body. She was told that because of prayer she had been given an extended period of life, but that because of her karma she would suffer for a while longer.

This did not make Tara feel any better; in fact, she was getting worse and worse and really felt abandoned by everyone and everything. Then, what she considers to have been a miracle happened. She was sitting in her screen house in her back yard reading. "I felt helpless and hopeless, and if I'd had a gun at that time I would have gladly killed myself," she says. "Then I read what was to be my miracle. It was a quote from Psalm 118:17 and it said, 'I shall not die, but live, and declare the works of the Lord.' "

Tara read it out loud again and again; she knew it was a message from God. She had reached that place called "the pits" and she was surrendering to God to do His work. She had studied religions, philosophies, psychology, self-help, holistic medicine, and anything metaphysical for thirty years, and suddenly she understood that God wanted her to use all that knowledge to help others—not the help she gave her mother that denied her own wellness, but the kind of help that comes from healthy people. She was to have compassion, not become a martyr. She was filled with hope.

Tara was not instantly healed. With her new insight, however, she was led to the right doctor, who immediately diagnosed her as having Parkinson's disease (PD) and gave her medicine. She started taking the medicine with hopeful feelings because she knew that God had a hand in her future and that she was finally on the right route to her own well-being.

First, Tara applied her knowledge of prayer, meditation, and visualization exercises on herself. She explains, "I put myself on many prayer lists, read everything I could on PD and surrendered myself to healing. In the meantime, I realized that people were coming to me more and more for help. Being a student and facilitator of *A Course in Miracles*, I knew about the Holy Spirit and I felt that I was being used to help these people by sharing my own hope."

Tara's body was getting stronger and stronger. She felt more alive than she had in years. At the time of her participation in the A.R.E. research project, her only remaining outward manifestation of the disease was in her hand, which still shakes occasionally, affecting her handwriting. But, she says, "I use my typewriter and I can do everything else. The doctor is amazed at how well the medicine worked for me, but I know it was my reliance on hope that helped me to succeed."

People who meet Tara now find it hard to believe that there is anything wrong with her; sometimes she even forgets that herself. She started holding meetings in her home twice a week. One is on the *Course in Miracles* and the other is on "self-help, in which I teach from all the beautiful teachers, including Edgar Cayce."

Tara tells us she is still looking forward to a complete healing, but until then, she adds, "I know I will always be taken care of and protected from anything that will hurt me. What a wonderful feeling it is to know that my life gives so many people the hope that their life can be turned around, just like mine."

* * *

Denise is a student of Native American spirituality, which served her well when her mother became ill. She was admitted to the hospital for chest pains. Five years before, she'd had quadruple bypass surgery, so this time the doctors decided to perform the routine tests (angiogram, EKG, etc.). The family was very concerned though not yet alarmed. During the angiogram, however, Denise's mother suffered heart failure and had to be put on artificial life support systems. Now the family was alarmed.

The doctor discovered that all her old bypass grafts had disintegrated due to her diabetes and that there were no strong arteries with which to work. He told his patient it was the end and that she should get her affairs in order.

Through all those painful hours and days, Denise just knew that despite the odds, it wasn't her mother's time to die. "I was hopeful throughout and I even started feeling stupid about it. I thought maybe it's just wishful thinking. My mom planned her funeral and, two days later, the doctor burst in with exciting news. He had gone over the heart test video and found an artery they could use. Although her surgery was extremely high risk, he felt it was worth it."

Her mother is now enjoying a complete recovery, and Denise's understanding of Native American spirituality proved to be the strongest hope for her mother's heart. She had been praying for her mother's recovery, and one night she got her answer. "I had a vision of the white buffalo as I awakened in the night. That is symbolic of an answer to prayer. I cried tears of joy and hope," she says.

* * *

Sometimes one dose of hope is not enough to heal. Sometimes it needs to be administered regularly over a long period of time before one sees the effects. This is the case with Lilian. "A long series of small miracles has given me new hope."

After her divorce, Lilian really felt like a failure. She left her church and friends and beautiful home behind in the South to move to Kansas to be near her parents. At first, all Lilian did was work to keep a roof over her head; her life was very sparse. She had always made friends easily and always seemed to attract the kindest people as friends, so she very quickly acquired a strong support group around her. Still, she wasn't truly happy. "I had never been really happy inside—not even when I was little."

In Kansas, she kept getting more and more tired, sick, and depressed all the time. Her physical appearance aged by about twenty years. She was so tired that she could hardly hold her head up. Everything hurt! But never bad enough that she couldn't work or smile or be cheerful, but bad enough that she didn't care about life any more. Her doctor said that she was working too hard and that she was getting old. He gave her so many kinds of medicine to patch up her failing systems that she lost track of the number. She turned forty but looked older than her seventy-six-year-old father "who looks fifty-five and has the energy of someone thirty."

Lilian started reading every medical book she could find. She kept coming across the name Edgar Cayce. This led her to the book *There Is a River* by Thomas Sugrue. She had always considered herself to be a spiritual seeker but reading that book changed her life. "It was as if I had been groping my way through a dark and unfamiliar place and suddenly someone turned all the lights on so that I could not only see where I was going, but I could also watch my steps carefully and make it safely." That book about Cayce helped Lilian get back on spiritual searching ground again. She stopped thinking about her physical health and started thinking about her soul. Oddly enough, when this happened, the answers started coming to her about her health! She began to feel hope.

A friend gave her a book called *The Yeast Connection* by William G. Crook, about a condition called *Candida albicans.* Her doctor said that was what he had been testing her for and gave her more medicine. She got a little better, then much worse. She had gained a lot of weight. She was so stiff she couldn't touch her toes, turn her head left or right, or lift her arms above her chest without pain. She had pain and swelling in all her joints, a constant sore throat, and ear infections. Lilian was so weak and tired, and again could hardly hold her head up. Now, she was more hopeless than ever.

One day she went into a health-food store in her hometown to buy a candy bar and instead spotted a flyer on *Candida.* She asked the owner about it and was told to talk to Helen. When she found Helen, Lilian looked at the beautiful, young woman in front of her and wondered how she could possibly be of help. But Helen's story of illness and despair hit very close to home. Instead of a candy bar, Lilian left with a book called *The Yeast Syndrome* by John Parks Trowbridge and Morton Walker, plus $157.00 worth of vitamins and nutrients!

Ironically, she had spent that much on medicine two months in a row, but decided it was worth a try. Two days later, she could turn her head for the first time in months without moving her whole body. The doctor hadn't even been able to adjust her spine for two years because she was so stiff and sore. He kept saying that he was afraid he'd break something if he tried too hard. Now her back is almost perfect.

Since the day that Lilian talked to Helen she has kept to the four-step diet plan in the book and faithfully taken her vitamins! "The change is such a miracle and so obvious that everyone in town is noticing, and many are trying the treatment themselves with equally wonderful success," and adds, "The excess weight has fallen off like magic. I again have the strength, stamina, muscle tone, and flexibility that I had as a teen. People are again saying to me, 'You have a twenty-seven-year-old son? You don't look that old yourself!' And this time around, I believe they are sincere, because the mirror is again showing me a young-looking face."

Some days she still aches and has setbacks because her system is still healing itself, but she now has the strength to care about others and help them when they need her. "My poor health led me to the work of Edgar Cayce, which led me to spiritual hope, which led me to health. All of this will give me the chance to lead others down the same joyful path! Life is very good!"

✳ ✳ ✳

Carrie tells us a story of healing hope that was strong enough to save a child's life. She and Chuck were blessed with the premature arrival of a three-pound twelve-ounce little girl. Their new daughter seemed quite normal and they were able to take her home from the hospital as soon as she weighed four-and-one-half pounds. After three months of living at home with a very unhappy infant who was misdiagnosed as having mere colic, the new parents were at the end of their patience and energy and hope. Baby Michele still only weighed five-and-one-half pounds and was admitted to the hospital with a diagnosis of "failure to thrive."

Due to an esophageal reflux (food reentering the esophagus instead of flowing to the stomach), immediate surgery was scheduled. The doctors inserted a central IV line and placed a gastrotube in Michele's stomach through which Carrie and Chuck would feed their baby for the next year. They were told that if the G-tube came out, it was to be put back in immediately or the hole would close and Michele would then need another operation.

A year later the G-tube was removed by the doctor, but the hole didn't heal. Eight months later the hole in Michele's stomach was still open, and her parents were told that another operation would be needed to close it. Surgery was scheduled for two weeks later.

The night before surgery, Carrie had the terrible feeling that Michele would not survive the procedure. She stayed up most of the night praying, using a bottle of holy water, and trying her own hands-on healing. "I sent energy through my hands to Michele's wound and prayed that God would close the hole to her stomach." Although in the morning Carrie sensed new hope for Michele and her future, she says, "My husband felt I had lost my mind."

While driving to the hospital, Carrie mentioned to Chuck that she hadn't seen anything seeping out of the hole that morning, but he laughed and said, "It's wishful thinking. Do you honestly think that hole could close in one night with a prayer when it's stayed open for eight months already?" Carrie said yes. She thought for a moment that perhaps he was right. However, since the surgery was all set up, they figured they ought to have it done because it was probably just her imagination.

Right before the anesthesiologist started work on Michele, Carrie calmly mentioned the fact that she thought the hole looked different to her and asked if the surgeon could please look at it. Chuck cast her an unpleasant look and rolled his eyes, but she insisted on waiting for the doctor. Her healing hope could not be squelched this time by Chuck or by anyone else.

To Carrie's utter delight the doctor said that indeed the opening was no longer there. Surgery was cancelled and they were sent home. Carrie had been a part of the miracle of healing. She had used herself and her belief in prayer to help her daughter get well. The hope inside of her had been awakened and called to service.

* * *

Janis was in her thirties when she finally became hopeful about her own health care. It occurred after a year of suffering from chronic pain in her right lower back area. Physical therapy did not seem to alleviate the pain. Four doctors gave her different opinions of the problem. She went to see still another doctor who scheduled her for a CAT scan of the abdomen.

Two days after the CAT scan, Janis received a call at work from the most recent doctor. The news was not good. There was a large mass in the area where she had been experiencing pain. The doctor was ninety-nine percent sure that the mass was malignant. Janis immediately left work in a state of shock. During the bus ride home, all she could think of was, "How long do I have?" She was admitted to the hospital the next day for more tests, and they scheduled surgery for that next week.

Two nights before her surgery, Janis had a dream. In the dream, she recalls vividly seeing her paternal grandfather and many other people who had long since passed away. She reached to embrace her grandfather and felt a warmth emanating from him. Suddenly, he pushed her away from him and started to retreat back into a bright light. Janis sensed that he was saying to her, "It is not your time." The next day after she was admitted into the hospital, she told her mother about the dream. Her mother immediately told Janis that her dream meant she should be hopeful. Shortly after that the surgeon came in to discuss what her chemotherapy options would be following the surgery; he also told her to have hope. Janis thought they were both crazy. "What is hope?" she thought to herself. "How can I have hope—this is an awful, tormenting experience for me."

Late the next night, after she had started to drift into sleep, Janis was awakened by the phone at her hospital bedside. It was the surgeon. "I am sending you home tomorrow," he said. Janis immediately thought, "They want me to have hope, yet they can't even help me." To her surprise, he added, "Further tests have shown that this mass is nothing but fluid. You have no cancer." "I was so overjoyed and relieved—it is beyond words," Janis exclaims. "The experience still haunts me, but now I believe there is always hope."

＊ ＊ ＊

These stories all encourage us to recognize hope as a natural, high-potency medicine—our own power to heal. They show us that there are internal ways to fight disease, but that it requires concentration, an understanding of your ailment, and utilizing your own hope. Consider the possibility of combining the best medical technology and expertise of trained health care professionals with your own supply of healing hope. How do you feel now?

9

HOPE

IS HUMBLE

" . . . that each soul may,
too, take hope; may, too,
be just kind, just gentle,
just patient, just humble."

Based on Edgar Cayce Reading 518-2

The humble side of hope has no ego. It modestly emerges as a commonplace and unassuming resource in all our lives. There are no bells and whistles with this kind of hope; it simply emerges when you may be trying too hard on your own. When you're too deeply engrossed in your own pain, hope surfaces to "bring you up short" and put you in your place. It gives you permission to give up the fight and give control back to God.

❋ ❋ ❋

When Tony was quite young, he had arthritis in his right

knee. His hope was that he would outgrow it. He didn't. He had hoped that surgery would help and had agreed to two operations to break the adhesions that had formed on his knee. But the surgery did nothing to free his rusted knee joint. As a result, he spent many months in casts. After each operation, however, he would try to work harder at moving his knee and always hoped that his effort would help, but it had no effect.

Tony missed a lot of school during those years. Consequently, he was behind his peers. Still, he believed that getting healthy was his most important goal. He kept on hoping and kept on eating a cereal called Pablum® as part of his diet.

Somehow in the midst of all these approaches his grandmother, without ever saying anything, began gently massaging his leg daily. "I held out very little hope for this treatment, considering that if all the other stuff they tried did not cause an improvement, this wouldn't either." Gradually, however, something happened. The swelling subsided, the tightness under his knee became more flexible. It became possible to move his knee up and down a tiny bit without pain.

Although there was some small improvement, he began to have what he calls "an ambivalent feeling of helplessness." In retrospect, he feels that if he had been courageous enough to have more upbeat feelings, he could have helped himself more and would have had a smoother time of it. "But," he says, "that was then, this is now." He was too busy hoping for the wrong things. Through it all, Tony's grandmother never uttered one word about her feelings, about her dread, or about her hope. Without a trace of self-importance, she just kept quietly massaging his leg.

After a little over a year, Tony was able to proudly take a ten-step walk from the hallway out onto the front porch. He can still remember the wonderful feeling of being upright, mobile, and free with no cast. Again, grandmother never said a thing. She just went back to her chore of canning the family's winter food supply.

Tony's pain and the loss of youthful fun can only be imagined. The casts put on his leg were cumbersome and difficult to handle, and all the efforts his parents put forth had only limited success. "They tried terribly hard to help. Yet, grandmother made all her efforts seem common and reserved."

Grandmother's daily massaging was, to Tony, passionless and free from pride. She remained unchanged by either his success or his struggles. She never acknowledged the part she played in his first ten steps, yet it was through her humble hope that Tony was able to walk.

It took a long time for him to realize who had the greater measure of hope and, more important, who had channeled that hope into action. What his grandmother did seemed so natural at the time that now Tony says, "I'm not sure I ever formally thanked her. With a basic feeling of hope and help, and an understanding far beyond me, grandmother started me on the road to walking normally."

❊ ❊ ❊

The humble side of hope surfaced for Colleen and her husband when their son, Peter, was in his late twenties. He was an admitted alcoholic. Though he was going through the motions of sobriety, he was still dependent on his parents. Always in debt, he finally lost his driver's license because he had no insurance. For the next year he became even more dependent on Mom and Dad. The future looked grim for all of them.

Colleen practiced meditation with affirmations every chance she could. Her main affirmation was, "Something good will come from this." One day as she was alone driving in the car, she was overwhelmed by a feeling of love for her troubled Peter. From somewhere deep inside she received the message that told her to stop worrying about him and to "just love him." Through the message, she had been directed to let go of Peter's problems and take charge of her own behavior. This was a humbling realization for a mother who was trying to be all things to him. This was very difficult for her to do, but she heeded her hopeful message.

Sure enough, during this time of letting go, Colleen saw her son begin to mature and slowly heal. Within six weeks, he had found an apartment that was walking distance to his job. Although Colleen continued to take him to most of his A.A. meetings, he started to go to a few on his own. Two years later Colleen had a son who was quite independent and caring. Besides his A.A. meetings, Peter now attends church regularly. "He still has problems," says Colleen, "but *he's* dealing with them." One day at a time, Colleen is reminded of the humble hope that was rekindled within her on that lonely ride in her car. She learned to give Peter his own problems back so that he could learn to deal with them. Her humble awakening of hope simply said to love him. And she did.

* * *

Humble hope emerges when you are lost in your own despair or when you're drowning in misery. But instead of dramatically yanking you to your senses, it merely appears as a matter-of-fact reminder that you need to take a practical look at your own situation. Hope recently encouraged a woman named Sharon to simply "blink your eyes and look again. Things could be much worse." Sharon was at the lowest point in her life. At forty, her husband of twenty years declared his love for another woman. Soon after, he left her and their two teen-age daughters. She was miserable.

Every day she cried on her half-hour ride to work. She was afraid, alone, and resentful of the other woman. One day in her car she suddenly heard a little voice say, "Look around. You have much to be happy and thankful for at this moment." She was startled and wondered how anything could be more important than her own pain. She felt as if someone had rapped the back of her hand and said, "Stop this nonsense!" What she really felt was the humble tap of hope that reminded her to stop focusing on her self and to look outside of her own pain. She did look around. She noticed that it was a sunny spring morning. Flowers were blooming and the birds were singing. When she really thought about it, her body felt good. There were no aches or pains. With humility she agreed, "Yes, I do have much to be happy and thankful for."

Hope helped her to move beyond her feelings of despair and to focus on what was pleasant in life, like the trees, the birds, and the flowers. She said that after that reminder, "I thought about living in the now instead of looking back at the past which I was blaming for my misery. That was the last day I cried on my drive to work." Hope helped Sharon to stop feeling sorry for herself and to take responsibility for her own happiness. As the weeks and months passed, she began to know that whatever should happen, "be it ever so terrible, my future will include happiness."

The next time you're feeling down try to do what Sharon did. Take a look around you, look up at the sky, breathe the air, think about how you really feel without fear or sorrow. Decide to encourage hope into your life by listening to your inner voice. Quiet your mind for a moment and hear the humble side of hope speak.

✳ ✳ ✳

In 1966, after completing four years of honorable service to his country, Kent was discharged from the U.S. Air Force. Immediately, he began to search for civilian employment in order to provide for his wife and infant son.

That search led him to a position as a shipping clerk in a local kitchen cabinet manufacturing firm in Sioux City, Iowa. The pay was very low and the conditions were extremely depressing and uncomfortable, but he worked hard with the hope of improving his situation. That hope sprang from what he says was an indescribable, persistently present feeling. It was nurtured by his longstanding belief that "If a person will humble himself and work at the most distasteful of tasks within an organization, then he or she will ultimately realize advancement within the organization."

Eventually, Kent was promoted to the position of executive credit manager. New challenges arose. "The job was more difficult because the business was growing and struggling. Management was headstrong, stubborn, and independent. Many of my decisions were shoved aside, and the management took risks that later proved to be disadvantageous to the whole enterprise."

Kent's difficulties were compounded when he realized that the pay level for his new position would remain low and that there was little promise of further advancement. He had a title, but little authority to accomplish the long-term objectives of either the company or himself. It was a "Catch-22" situation, and it became increasingly frustrating with the passing of time. Yet, he held on faithfully for seven more years—until 1973.

Simultaneously, Kent began to search for another job and look inwardly for answers. He also had a part-time job in a local night club at what he calls a "table-hopping psychic doing character readings and prognostications for the customer's entertainment." The lounge job was a source of deeper frustration. He knew he was abusing his gift of insight for the sake of shallow entertainment. "There was little substance to the advice I gave to the clientele there."

A crisis was fast approaching in his employment situation as well as his personal well-being. His finances were not adequate to sustain his family and the threat of bankruptcy loomed. Something had to be done, but he had no idea of what to do. One night, he finally reached the depths of despair. He went home, exhausted from a day's work at the factory and a night's work at the night club.

Sprawled on his bed, he prayed to God for help. He explains, "I was as humble as a child when I acknowledged my need for guidance. It was a selfish prayer perhaps, but I said, 'God, I am making no more than $120 per week at work and almost nothing at the night club. I need a job that will pay $300 per week.'"

That very same evening, two significant things happened to him. First, he had a vivid dream—or vision—of an angel who said to him, "The gift of insight has been given to you by God, and you are no longer to use it for the mere entertainment of others." Secondly, at 3:30 a.m., there was a knock on his front door. It was an old air force buddy who had come from Michigan. "You are coming with me to Detroit," he informed Kent, "and you are going to go to work with me at the automobile plant." To Kent, this visit was totally unannounced and unexpected, but, of course, it was no surprise to the humble side of hope that had just been patiently waiting to answer his prayer.

Kent immediately packed a bag, told his wife what was happening, got into the automobile with his friend, and headed for the new job. In less than a week, he was making the necessary $300 per week and more. "The money was great, but the challenge of properly managing so much more money than I had ever had before was difficult and later proved to be impossible." Through ignorance, he and his family lived "high on the hog" from 1973 until 1978. "We lived selfishly. We lived for the next paycheck. Money became our motivation for living."

Caught in a vicious trap of excess and a lack of humility, Kent turned to illicit drugs. This eventually led to bankruptcy, the loss of his job, and a criminal record for being caught selling illegal substances to his co-workers. When the treadmill stopped and Kent looked at the mess he had created, he said to himself, "God gave me a great blessing and I blew it." His family left him and returned to Iowa to fare as best they might. Kent remained in Detroit, destitute, demoralized, ill, and transient. He says, "It seemed that life was over for me and that there was no hope of a future. Darkness prevailed over every aspect of my life. Out on parole, I was literally forced to sleep in wooded areas and under bridges. I was sick and homeless, while one door after another seemed to slam shut in my face."

At the moment of his deepest despair, he met a Christian man who listened to, prayed with, and counseled him. He rekindled Kent's focus on God, helping him to think of God once again as forgiving and sustaining. In time and with the help of his new friend, Kent began to let go of his misery and refused to attach further conditions on his own future to God.

A humble hope was rekindling, but he had no idea what to hope for. He had no energy left for being a part of the process of his own future. Finally he was willing to simply "rest in the back of the boat and let God do the steering." He concludes, "This kind of resignation takes courage, but if the person is willing to espouse complete, dedicated, and utterly blind faith in God, there is a spiritual force that will reinforce it."

Finally, Kent's experiences from the past were beginning

to make a positive impact on his future. This time he was really letting go, for good. During this trying period, two jobs opened for him. One was in a Christian bookstore and the other was in a convenience store. Soon afterward, the convenience store was destroyed in a tornado, so the choice was easy. It was later that year while Kent was working at the Christian bookstore that he had an experience that was to change his life again. A woman came in and began talking to him about God and healing. She had a copy of *A Seer Out of Season: The Life of Edgar Cayce* by Harmon Hartzell Bro, Ph.D., and gave Kent the book as a gift of love.

He took the book and started reading "little snatches of it here and there." As he was reading, he had an overwhelming urge to leave Michigan at once and go back home. He felt he had to do this even if it meant walking the whole distance from Detroit to Sioux City. "And," he adds, "I was determined to do exactly that if need be."

He did return to Sioux City and reconciled with his family. However, they lived in what he describes as a "roach-eaten apartment in a neighborhood that had been previously flooded out. The area was filled primarily with the poor, the degenerate, the alcoholic, and the doper." Yet it also rested on the banks of the wide and peaceful Missouri River. This thick ribbon of water that runs through Sioux City's roughest section symbolized for Kent a thing of beauty. It became what he calls his "key of hope and salvation in desperation."

He would spend hours beside that thick river, silently listening to the inner voice of God within him. It was a time of relief from his burdens. He was humbled by the peaceful power of the river which just kept flowing no matter what Kent was feeling or doing, seemingly unaffected by his presence. "It was a spiritual oasis in the desert of my afflictions." That river was the catalyst for hope that would free him once and for all from the horrors of the past several years.

On the banks of that river an idea came to Kent, seemingly from nowhere, to appeal to the U.S. government for help in his desperate situation. It led him to the phone book and to the Comprehensive Employment Training Act (C.E.T.A.) offices in Des Moines. That led him through a training program and ultimately back to Sioux City to the job he has held now for the past ten years—a job that completely reestablished him financially and helped to restore him physically, spiritually, and emotionally.

No longer a young man, Kent is now a better man. His experiences with humble hope have helped him to let go of his struggles and to enjoy the many gifts he has received—first from a dream, then a friend, then a book, and finally a river. He concludes, "Today, the shadows of the dismal past no longer touch me. I am made whole. I am happy."

✳ ✳ ✳

Maureen had just found out that her husband was being unfaithful to her in the worst way. He was seeing her best friend, a situation she says she will never forget. It threw her into a state of tears and depression that she had never experienced before or since.

She had been crying for days and could not eat. She had just sent her children to school and sat down at the table to cry once more. Her heart was broken and she felt there was nothing that would ever lift this sadness from her. But, she adds, " I was wrong. In my left ear I heard the actual voice of my deceased mother. Some people would say I had this experience because I had not eaten. Nonsense. I'm a down-to-earth person who does not see or hear things that are not there. Very clearly, my mother said, in a voice that started far away and ended far away, 'Maureen, stop it.' Suddenly, everything else was a minor problem by comparison."

She knew at that instant that there is much more beyond the life we live on earth, that there is a life after death. Maureen, like Sharon, felt the tap of hope that reminds us all to move on with our lives and to stop feeling sorry for ourselves. It's humbling to have the power of our pain suddenly turn to dust, to be reminded to "shape up and fly right." But it can work for all of us just like it worked for Sharon and Maureen. Maureen got right up, ate a bowl of oatmeal that morning, and started on the road to recovery. "For the past twenty-five years since this happened to me," she explains, "whenever things get me down, I remember my mother's sweet voice in my ear."

Her experience with hope was brief but lasting. Her mother's humble message reminds all of us that our own pain is a small part of the whole picture of our lives, and when it is time to move on, we must do so.

✳ ✳ ✳

Think for a moment of a person you might know who is like Tony's grandmother. Someone who is short on words; yet who, without ceremony, simply and quietly does the right thing. We can't all be like that. We are who we are. Yet Tony's grandmother represents the part of all of us that is humble—the part of us that knows what to do, does what's right, and doesn't expect any rewards. Hope quietly encourages us to go on with the business of living a good life.

We can exercise that humble part of us, like Sharon did, by putting limits on our pain and then sending it on its way. The first step is to let go of the struggle and walk away from the fight. Kent, like the rest of the people in the stories, finally gave up his struggle and is now free of pride. It's not easy to let go of your own pain. Pain is very powerful and consuming, but hope is there to fill the void. Hope rushes in the moment that you consider another point of view—a point of view triggered by a simple thought, a gentle voice, or a common gesture. It's the kind of hope that encourages you to take a deep breath, look again at your life, and loosen your grip on your own despair. Don't be afraid; you won't be left empty-handed—you will quickly feel a handshake from the humble side of your own hope.

10
HOPE
IS HUMOROUS

*"Hope feels like a
small rubbery core
inside me that will keep
bouncing back forever."*

Mary North of Riner, Virginia

Laughter is a direct message to the universe. It announces a temporary truce, a momentary letting go of our fear, pain, and resentment. Not to be confused with surrender or resignation, laughter is a comic relief from those thoughts that can make us sad or unhealthy. In that deep breath that follows a giggle, a chuckle, or a great belly laugh, hope can scoot in and make things better, leaving a smile in its wake.

✳ ✳ ✳

About six months before Denise was to be married, her future brother-in-law, Buddy, went into the hospital for a liver transplant. He was young and in good shape, so his prognosis was good and family hopes were high. In August, four months and three transplants later, Buddy died, surrounded by his family and a medical staff that had quickly grown to love him for his courage and good nature.

Denise recalls this story in terms of her experience with hope, yet it's also about Buddy's hope. She visited him almost every day and almost every time she would find him lying there in his bed in his hospital gown—and jogging shoes! His doctors told him that wearing them would keep his feet at a 90° angle and prevent his Achilles tendons from shortening and his muscles from atrophying.

But Denise knew another reason for Buddy wearing those shoes. It was his pride and his sense of humor. "He was showing his hope that death wasn't an ending, but a step to be prepared for. He was going to be dressed for the next life." Because Buddy's hope was so good-natured and light-hearted, his death did not feel like a defeat to his family. Very sad, of course, but not a failure.

Denise's wedding was not canceled or even postponed. She was a beautiful, happy bride because she knew that Buddy would want her to be. "I learned from him that hope has nothing to do with things going your way and that death isn't something you take your shoes off for!"

* * *

Hope has a way of opening up your heart and letting good feelings rush in. You can't stop the flow of fun when you're laughing. Hope bolts past the thoughts and notions that have been making you sad, afraid, or sick, and it has a way of making you forget your despair so that you can begin to repair your life.

Twenty years ago a nurse named Shelly contracted hepatitis from one of her patients. The disease became chronic, and she was sick for the next three years. At one point, the illness was so severe that the doctor pronounced it "chronic aggressive" rather than "chronic persistent." That meant that she would have less than three years to live.

The medication she took gave her adverse reactions, so finally she discontinued using it. Her despair and anger were tremendous. She was resentful that she had become ill in the process of caring for someone else, and she had become terribly discouraged that modern medicine was not helping her at all.

"Then, I stumbled upon a rerun of *Burns and Allen,* the old Gracie Allen and George Burns television show. I started to laugh, and hope immediately began to enter my life. A few nights later I watched Gilda Radner on *Saturday Night Live*—and more laughter. The next week I started to pray and finally came the first signs of remission." Shelly believes her remission was triggered by her laughter—a letting go, a relaxation of her grief, and a rest from her resentment; just long enough to let in some hope. It made her strong and well enough to begin to repair her body. Her first step back to wellness was laughter.

Once her disease was in remission she ought to have taken an inventory of the other damage due to unhealed emotional scars. For example, she didn't have the luxury of really exploring her resentments—she had too many bills to pay and, therefore, had to begin looking for work right away. It had been a long time since she had done this, and she encountered great difficulty in going back to patient care because of what she went through during her own illness.

She finally got a job in a public detox center and was relieved that she would be working again to start paying off her bills. "What I didn't count on was what I would learn from my new patients. They helped me begin to look at myself in a new light. They helped me learn that I am powerless over many things, including my hepatitis. I learned to trust my higher power. Because of my remission I felt for the first time in my life that I would never be alone again and that there is always hope." It was laughter that triggered Shelly's remission and made her strong and well enough to go back to work. When she began to relate to her new patients, her own real healing began.

✻ ✻ ✻

The humorous side of hope followed Joe all the way to graduate school. He had given himself a huge challenge, which he was taking too seriously, so humorous hope emerged to tickle his funny bone when he was all alone in his dorm. Joe purposely ventured off to a graduate school where he didn't know a soul. He had always been outgoing, and his personal history assured him that he would make many new friends and adjust easily. Yet it turned out that his choice resulted in a very lonely and distressing year, until he started to smile.

Right after school started, Joe recognized that he was unhappy and actively searched for the answer to how he could regain his joyful disposition. He tried talking to other students, even teachers, about this dilemma but no one seemed to have the solution. This went on for well over a year. Then one night at Christmas, alone in his room, he turned on the television and began to watch "Ziggy's Christmas," a cartoon show based on the comic strip character Ziggy by Tom Wilson. By the time that simple, silly one-hour cartoon was over, Joe realized he had been smiling the whole time and that he had thoroughly enjoyed himself. He also knew that the answer to his loneliness had come from the cartoon story. As he thought about it, he realized that he was to "Give Joy."

Joe sat there stunned as he realized that this would be his solution. He had been so busy looking for ways to become happy that he had forgotten to reach out to others and to give. He had spent so much of his energy focusing on his own unhappiness that he was surprised at how easy it was to be happy. "It was suddenly so clear and I was filled with hope."

His new hope stayed with him. He went back to those people from whom he had sought answers, only this time he gave joy. Now in their thirties, those people are still his close friends. As a matter of fact, one of them became his wife. "They were there all along," Joe says, "but I couldn't see that until I started giving of myself."

As he looks back, he feels that the whole process was very spiritual. He believes that it was necessary for his growth and development, and he still smiles every year when he sees "Ziggy's Christmas."

❋ ❋ ❋

The essence of humor comes from a sense of the ridiculous and the unpredictable. Something may be funny because it is out of context, unexpected, or decidedly out of the ordinary. Recognizing the irony and humor of a situation is the first step to having a good hopeful laugh.

Gerti was walking down the street enjoying the day when a pleasant-faced, elderly woman whom she'd never seen before stopped her and said, "This is the first time I've had a chance to thank you for sending the card when my husband died."

Gerti lives in a high-rise condominium complex with 253 condos, and she frantically searched her mind to place the woman. "As one who lives in this village of homes stacked on top of each other, I have sent cards to a lot of the people—birthday cards, get-well cards, sympathy cards, and thank-you notes for the many gestures of kindness shared by my neighbors. Why was this woman stopping me and who was the man to whom she was referring?"

"I'm John's mother," she said. "My husband died about
five months ago. Remember?" Of course, Gerti remembered
John, the woman's son, as one of the younger homeowners,
a wealthy bachelor who used his condo on the New Jersey
shore as a retreat from his busy life as an investment broker.
That settled, she was ready to be on her way when the
widow began to chat. First, she told Gerti that her name was
Bernice. She mentioned how good John had been to his father before he died, taking him to Europe where "Daddy,"
as she affectionately called him, had the time of his life. He'd
also let his father use his condo as often as he wished.

She rambled on and on, and Gerti began to get restless
and shift her weight from one foot to the other. Bernice continued. "Daddy had a terrible sickness. He had what's called
scleroderma. Then he got other complications. He eventually had to have a leg removed. It was just awful. He went
into cardiac arrest several times. The last time it happened,
when I called the medics, they said he was gone."

Bernice's eyes filled with tears as she recalled her pain.
She searched her pockets for a tissue, then Gerti handed
her one. "I prayed all the way to the hospital. 'O Lord, don't
take him now,' I kept saying. 'We love each other so much.'
He was put in the emergency room and after working on
him for a long time the doctors got him breathing again.
Eventually they took him to the intensive care unit. I was so
happy. I was crying like a fool. You know, we'd been married
fifty-one years and he was a good man."

Gerti was nodding her head patiently as Bernice continued. "He came to, but I'd never seen him act that way before.
He was madder than a wet hen. I couldn't imagine what had
gotten into him. You'd a'thought he'd be real thankful for
being alive, but not him. He ranted and raved, especially at
me. I hollered for the nurse! 'Why did they keep pounding
on my chest?' he was scolding. 'I didn't want none of it. I
knew where I was at. I was in heaven. I saw the most beau-

tiful, shiny places. I saw more folks we know, those that have gone on. I never wanted to come back.' "

At the image of the outrageous scene of this angry man, sputtering about being brought back, and poor Bernice grieving so, Gerti couldn't help but start to chuckle. She thought to herself, "Who ever heard of such a thing?" She pictured Bernice pulling her husband back to life with his feet dragging like a reluctant child, and she couldn't stifle her laugh.

Gerti reached over and put her arms around Bernice. Soon they were both laughing about the irony. Bernice thought for a minute, and then smiled as she finished her story. Daddy had said to her with great annoyance, "They told me I had to. I had to come back and tell others that there is no death. That life goes on . . . " Daddy died one week later—this time without a fight.

After her story was finished, Gerti watched Bernice leave in silence. They were no longer strangers. They had shared a very private moment. Bernice didn't realize that she had left Gerti with a hopeful and humorous story about life on the other side. As Gerti opened the door to her building, she knew she had a gift she could share with her friends and neighbors for many years to come.

✻ ✻ ✻

Humorous hope, of course, emerges in different people in different ways, but it was about to make a hilarious visit to some stranded and very cool teen-aged boys. Corrine had decided to take her three sons and their three friends up to the mountains on a skiing trip. Their ages ranged from nine to seventeen. It was, for most of them, their first ski trip. They drove to one of the boys' grandmother's cabin and slept the night in order to get an early start on the slopes the next day.

Bright and early the following morning the six boys piled into the car only to find it iced solid onto the driveway. It took forty-five minutes, with all boys shoveling to get it out. Once under way, the travelers wound slowly through the hills until they came to the main road. Corrine tried to accelerate but found that the car would not go any faster than ten to fifteen miles per hour. Finally, she stopped. They all got out and discovered that the right rear wheel was not moving at all. It was frozen in place.

There they were on Sunday morning in the mountains, in the middle of nowhere, and miles from the ski lodge. Some motorists drove by suggesting that her bearings had locked up. One even offered to call a tow truck for them when he got to the next phone. Corrine, who was almost 200 miles from home with six disappointed boys, didn't like her options. She feared a costly repair job with no way to get home until the repairs were done.

She thought a moment, took a deep breath, and said to the brokenhearted boys, "Get in the car. We're going to try something. We're going to meditate." The boys roared with laughter. They began wisecracking and shoving and teasing each other until they finally settled down. In the quiet that followed, Corrine taught them an exercise she had learned.

She led them through deep breathing, then progressive muscle relaxation. It was so quiet she could hear their hearts beating. When she counted to three, Corrine asked them to picture on a mental screen in front of their faces exactly the way the wheel looked—not turning. She had them put an "X" on the picture to get rid of it. On their mental screens they were to project another picture. This time they would see the wheel slowly beginning to turn, until finally it was completely turning and they were all moving along on their way to the ski slopes.

Lastly, she had them picture themselves skiing and having a marvelous day. When they opened their eyes, Corrine said, "Now I'm going to start the car, the wheel is going to turn, and we're going to have a wonderful day on the slopes." She remembers that "The energy in the car was busy and jovial. I put the key in the ignition, put my foot on the gas—we all heard a POP!—then the wheel began to turn, and we were on our way to a perfect day.

"The whole incident delayed us for only two hours, but there was not a kid in that car who wasn't happy to have had that experience. Their energy was so strong, they were so together. They spent the rest of the day in pure joy. There was not a doubt for me that once they had a good laugh to open them up, their focused hope, desire, and expectations had moved that wheel."

*　*　*

Judith has a powerful story about humorous hope that seemed to fly into her life and literally sit on her head to make her believe that fun is a fundamental part of a healthy life. Overwhelming pain awakened her one night, racking her body from head to foot. "It tore at my gut, throbbed in my head, and seared down my spine to my leg." In that pain she suddenly wondered how long she had been taking her health for granted. Evidently all her life, she thought. She was going to need some humor to help her with this kind of pain.

At the time, her life was a mess and she felt that she had nothing to hope for. She had recently left her home and a twenty-five-year marriage. Her father had just died, now she was alone and sick. Her will could not make the pain go away, nor could it ease the terror she felt when she was told there were tumors growing in her pelvic region and in her breast. She could not relax her spasming and irritated colon, and she could not renew her waning energy as she dragged herself through the days.

Never having felt this kind of pain before, she refers to it as a "rude awakening" and explains, "The comfortable dream state that I had encased myself in for forty-five years had suddenly been shattered by demons that tormented my physical, emotional, and mental body. I could no longer be wrapped in the slumber of denial and forgetfulness. The pain was too great. I had to wake up."

Judith was forced to ask herself, "How does one cope with such physical agony?" She had no idea. All her life she had been blessed with extremely good health and abundant energy. So good, in fact, that she had little patience with herself or with others who might be suffering this mysterious ailment that was beginning to change her life and threaten her future.

Seemingly she had been spared emotional pain, too. In the past, when something fearful confronted her, she had become an expert at ignoring it. She didn't have to endure the hurt or pain on an emotional level because, she sternly reasoned with herself, she would be all right as long as she buried those feelings and did not let them manifest in tears or anger. Like many women from the fifties generation, Judith grew up believing that, if she stayed in control, she could bring peace and comfort to herself and to those around her.

Coming from a medical family, she was sure that there was a magic pill or operation that would cure her. She went to all the practitioners. After months of painful regimens and exams, she realized that she was not improving. In fact, she was far worse than before. She started both group and private psychotherapy. She was seeing two different chiropractors and was consuming a concoction made for her by an herbologist. She would feel some relief for a few days, but the symptoms would always return. Even with all her efforts, she felt no hope.

By now her intestines were in such distress that eating had become a nightmare. She seemed to react negatively to everything she ate; thus, she developed the belief that she was allergic to most foods. She was literally starving to death and totally frustrated at what action to take next. "I finally realized that I had been addressing the physical, emotional, and mental aspects of my pain with my usual determination to control and conquer. Nothing was working. Now I couldn't even nourish my body. What else could I do?"

Consumed by that ferocious pain, Judith knelt down at the foot of her bed and cried out to God whom she was sure had deserted her. She sobbed uncontrollably. Finally she totally surrendered. Then an incredible thing happened. "A feeling swept through my battered body that was so strange it is difficult to describe. There were no visions, no voices from on high—but a feeling of calm and a deep knowing that in order to nourish and heal myself, I must address my spiritual starvation. I had been brought to my knees, weeping in pain and desperation, and for the first time in ages felt a deep peace surrounding me."

Judith had been attending meetings in a twelve-step program that spoke of "turning your life over to a power greater than yourself." Though the spiritual aspect of the program had alluded her, she had attended the meetings faithfully because she always left them with a somewhat peaceful feeling. Prayer along with meditation was another part of her journey to wellness, and Judith had started this practice very reluctantly. Yet to her amazement, during her periods of meditation, she was actually somewhat free from the chronic pain she suffered in her back and lower abdomen. Though she felt relief, she still felt no hope.

At this time she had also been introduced to a trance channeler who, it turned out, had gentle and loving messages for her. At first, she remained tremendously skeptical of the phenomenon. In spite of her own reserve, however, the messages resonated at a deep level of her being and calmed some of her fears. She had also mysteriously reconnected with a long-lost teaching colleague who brought her to a gifted psychic. Again Judith's intellect screamed at her, saying this was an absurd waste of time and money, but amazing shifts began to take place which she could not rationalize away.

Certain books began to find their way into her hands—given to her or recommended by friends, found abandoned at the laundromat, or seeming to reach out to her as she browsed in bookstores. One such book was Dr. Gerald Jampolsky's *Teach Only Love.* In this bright gem of a book, the author outlined the seven principles of healing found in the *Course in Miracles.* The one point that stood out above all others for Judith was to focus on achieving her own peace of mind. During this time of concentration, she was focusing on peace of mind, but not yet on hope.

Peace of mind was a quality that had eluded her from childhood. She had lived with alcoholism all her life. First her parents, then her husband, and finally her oldest son had all been diagnosed with this disease. She asked, "How could anyone feel peaceful when trying to control and manage loved ones who are suffering from alcoholism?"

The continuing pain forced her to focus on herself and to begin to nourish all those parts of her that she had neglected for so long. She began learning that the peace she was searching for was not outside of herself. No guru, channeled spirit, or psychic was going to be any more successful at giving her peace than the physicians, therapists, and chiropractors had been. Judith was beginning to realize that if she wanted a pain-free body, the healing had to come from within her.

But there was another important missing element. "In all my earnest efforts to look for solutions, I had forgotten how to play, how to find joy, how to have fun." Luckily, humor was soon to remind her that while she was on her quest for peace of mind and healing, she ought to learn not to take herself so seriously. Teaching youngsters at a public school, she has always enjoyed working with children and believes that their delightful energies help her to grow and learn. Little did she know that the lesson of hope through laughter would come from her own students.

One day the school invited a magician and his assistant to perform. They entertained in an enclosed area with room for about 200 children to sit crowded on the floor. Because there was no stage, an area in front of the room was cleared for them. The teachers, to save dignity and stiff joints, sat in folding chairs along the sides and back of the room. On this particular day Judith chose to sit in the back, happy at the opportunity for a moment to relax and watch someone else perform. Her high level of pain and low level of energy had really taken their toll on her enthusiasm for teaching her thirty-one youngsters.

As she watched the act, she was delighted that the magician was so proficient and the performance so professional. He had pulled the traditional white rabbit out of his top hat and performed some other wonderful routines with two beautiful white doves. At the conclusion of this part of the performance, he held the two doves in both hands, then threw them into the air above his head. With a flutter of wings one of the birds obediently settled into its cage at the magician's feet. The other, to everyone's astonishment, flew out across the room, circled around behind Judith, landed on her head—and just sat there!

The students were wildly laughing and pointing. The magician looked dismayed as his assistant went struggling through the sea of excited children to retrieve the errant bird. Afraid to move for fear of startling the poor creature, Judith just sat there with a dove perched atop her head, waiting to be rescued. The young assistant, with profuse apologies, lifted the creature from her head and returned it to its cage.

Finally, Judith started to laugh and continued to laugh for the rest of the day. The more she laughed, the more hopeful she became. The message to her was humorously clear that the missing piece in the puzzle was her joyful happiness. For her, the symbolism of the dove on her head meant that she had been given the gift of peace of mind. She had to laugh at what it took to trigger her hope—making her laugh so that she would stop taking herself and her path so seriously. It was time to find out what joy and laughter were all about. And, with new-found hope, she did.

"The progression of miracles in my life since that day are too numerous and lengthy to mention at this time. Suffice it to say, the pain of awakening has now been transformed into a joyous anticipation of what the next moment will bring. The humor that surrounds me and radiates from me is a source of wonder and hope to all—especially myself."

* * *

There is something special about a huge warm burst of laughter, letting go of control, and being just a little improper. But equally effective is just a simple smile. Cloie, who was walking home from work to her apartment in Chicago, had her hope awakened by a simple smile. Bracing herself against the city wind, she was bent forward with her arms wrapped around her purse. She had had a particularly awful day and she was fighting back tears of frustration.

She kept hearing a constant honking—not unusual in a big city—but there was something different about this particular honking; it seemed so urgent. When she looked for its source, she saw a large truck with three men cramped in the front seat. The driver was waving and smiling. Cloie looked around to see if there was anyone else to whom he might be signaling. Questions and answers raced through her mind:

Is he waving at me? Yes.

Do I know him? No.

What does he want from me? A smile.

He smiled back happily and drove off into the heavy traffic.

Cloie explains why that happy exchange renewed her hope: "I had just experienced God's use of one person to give another the perspective and understanding to carry on. Since then, I have felt as if I am part of God's family and that continues to keep me smiling."

✳ ✳ ✳

The playful side of hope can be triggered by a sincere smile or wave. But hope also responds to catastrophic incidents like when you've lost your job, your money, and worst of all, your self-esteem. At age fifty-seven, Jason became one of the many victims of a troubled economy. He lost his job due to cutbacks where he worked and so decided to move back home to Utah. He was depressed because of his serious economic difficulties and was praying and trying to think what to do next. When he finally fell asleep that night, he had a dream. In his dream, he was in a hotel room and through a door into the room walked, of all people, the comedian, Bob Hope!

After waking, Jason instantly recognized the humor in the symbolism of his dream. Its message to him was that his living situation was only temporary—because he was in a hotel—and his visit from Bob Hope meant that hope was coming into his life and would make him happy again. His hope was fulfilled a few days later in the form of a phone call and a job offer from a dear friend. Life for Jason is now working out well. He is still grateful for the way that hope, in the form of one of the world's greatest mirth-makers, was revived in him that night.

✳   ✳   ✳

Like Jason's dream message to be happy, humorous hope came to a young mother of three very late one night after much sorrow and confusion. For nearly thirty years Roberta has remembered reclaiming her own hope and the way it changed forever her life and the lives of her beloved family members.

By the time Roberta was twenty-eight years old, her life was so bleak that she had a nervous breakdown and attempted suicide four times. She was hospitalized and given shock treatments, but nothing really seemed to help. "I felt as though I were at the bottom of a deep well and could not get out. I didn't even have hope that I would ever want to get out."

Then she began to have dreams in which she would hear the telephone ring and, when she answered it, a voice would simply say, "God loves you." At this time, she was in a state of extreme self-hate. She saw everything in a negative light and had no humor at all—and certainly no hope.

One night during that state between awake and asleep, she heard three women's voices outside her bedroom window. They seemed to be having a great time, laughing and joking and carrying on. She realized that they were discussing her. At first she was upset, but then she had the feeling that they all loved her a great deal, even though they spoke of her as if she were a frustrated two-year-old child. They began to discuss what effect her illness was having on her husband and her children. Until this time Roberta was in such a darkened state that she never even considered that her family was in any pain at all.

One of the women said, "Boy, she is a hard nut to crack," and the other two went into peals of laughter. Then, another woman said, "If she would just develop a sense of humor." When Roberta awoke, she says, "I was full of hope. It was as though I had been born again. I had a purpose and a goal for which to live. I was going to find some humor in my life, and I was going to use the rest of my energy for my children and make sure that they would never experience anything like my deep depression."

She learned to regain her sense of humor and worked at finding and feeling the humorous side of life. She taught her children survival skills, like shopping, cleaning, and cooking. She taught them basically to be able to take care of themselves. They talked openly about everything, especially the difficult subject of sex.

Roberta continued to study everything she could get her hands on about depression and its causes. She participated in therapy groups and developed her sense of humor. She wasn't well all at once, however. She really had to grow and stretch a lot, but one day she realized that while her attention was on her children, making sure they felt supported and loved and had humor in their lives, somewhere along the line she was the one who was healed.

"My children are all grown and happy now. My husband and I are divorced, but remain good friends. I am very aware that as the *Course in Miracles* states, 'Happiness is my function.' The three women?—I think they are my guardian angels. I know I'm loved!" And now she is happy and full of hope.

✳   ✳   ✳

It's time to give laughter more respect, to see its purpose as a healthy tool for us to use in times of stress, despair, and disease. Try renting a funny video, going to a comic club, or watching a comedy show on television. Another way to get a good laugh or at least a smile is to browse the racks of humorous greeting cards. You might even find the perfect card to send to someone to restore hope. If none of this works, the surest place to find happiness is to go where children are laughing. No one can resist that kind of pure joy. You'll be very surprised at how good you will feel after just one chuckle.

The comedienne, Carol Burnett, once said that comedy was tragedy plus time. I suggest you don't wait for something terrible to turn into something funny. Give yourself the gift of laughter *right now.* If you do, you're doing much more than finding a smile, really. You'll be letting the Universe know that, despite it all, you're ready to welcome some hope into your life.

11
HOPE
IS RENEWABLE

*"Let love, life, and
hope be the motivating
forces in my thoughts and
acts day by day."*

Based on Edgar Cayce Reading 281-23

Like all the other colors of hope, renewable hope has certain identifiable features. It is recurring. It threads through our lifetime and beyond. Its triggers lie quietly in our memories in the form of colors, songs, words, and visions. Its roots are in more hopeful times—times of feeling especially loved, happy, or proud. Yet with carefully chosen thoughts that renew a hopeful experience, you can effectively harness today's depression and challenge tomorrow's despair.

* * *

Anais grew up in Norway in the fifties. At the time there

was a popular folk singer named Alf Proeysen. He had a style
of his own that touched her deeply; already, as a ten-year-
old girl, she felt especially drawn to his lyrics:
> "You shall receive a new day tomorrow
> that is clean and not used
> with shiny sheets and
> brand-new crayons . . ."

When Anais first heard those words, though she didn't
realize it, she had made a permanent friend of renewable
hope. As a youngster, whenever anything went wrong and
her day was damaged by unpleasant feelings or happen-
ings, she was reminded by the words to that song that
tomorrow would be a new day, that she could start the day
without any kind of "stains" either inside or outside her
heart. As an adult, she now realizes that the "brand-new
crayons" represent the many ways in which she has found
and used her own renewable hope.

The day she was diagnosed as having cancer in 1975, a
very close friend phoned her. The rain was pouring down,
and everything looked grey out on the landscape. Then he
said, "Remember, there is always much beauty in the grey
colors." Anais looked out the window and noticed that the
sun was sending little slivers of light through the clouded
sky and the calm fjord was indeed beautiful. She had found
another new crayon.

Five years later, she began having serious problems in her
marriage. One day another friend mentioned quietly, "The
green tree that bends its branches never cracks." She was
again reminded of her own supply of renewable hope and
found the will to go on.

Now she is back home in Norway after spending several
years in the United States. Her cancer has been in remission for almost twenty years and her marital problems have
been resolved. It's those colorful, recurrent messages of
hope that she has heard from several friends and a famous

singer that have kept her focused on tomorrow.

* * *

A senior citizen named Pearl has called upon her renewable hope throughout the nine decades of her life. When she was in junior high school, the country was in the throes of the Great Depression. She had been instructed in her sewing class to bring in material and a pattern for the next day. The teacher added that if students wanted to use their own bobbins provided for by the school, they would have to pay a dime for it.

Pearl went home with her instructions and her Aunt Meg said, "We don't have money for the bobbin, so you will have to share. I have a slip cut out for you, a nice flour sack with the letters boiled out of it. You could use that for your material."

She took what she calls her "prize" to school and recalls, "I don't think the teacher was prepared to handle that kind of a situation. She began sewing one seam, then let the stitching run off the side of the material, and got up saying, 'Hopeless, hopeless.' "

Confused and disappointed, Pearl went home and told Aunt Meg exactly what happened. First, Aunt Meg looked at the sewing and said, "Humph! She can't even sew a straight seam!" Then she looked at Pearl and said, "She didn't mean that you were hopeless. She meant that she thought your situation was hopeless. You can always change your situation, so don't ever feel hopeless about yourself."

Convinced that Aunt Meg was right, Pearl stayed in the sewing class and watched each demonstration that the teacher gave. She learned all she could, but did receive an "F" because she never sewed another item in that class.

During the many years since then, however, Pearl has sewn everything from drapes to seat covers to clothing.

Though she hadn't sewn lately, the most dramatic reminder of her hope came about two years ago (seventy years after that famous sewing class). She had been physically ill for quite some time. Though in her nineties, she refused to believe that her illness was age related. Finally, a doctor discovered that she was allergic to synthetics. The remedy??? Pearl is back to making her own clothes. She exclaims, "Thank God for sewing machines, cotton, wool, silk, and hope!"

* * *

Leah was twenty-one years old when she first discovered hope. She had been married for three years and was pregnant with her first child. She had wanted to have a baby for some time and was very excited when she learned of her pregnancy. The months that followed, however, were disappointing and difficult.

She was working full-time and was always exhausted. Her husband was looking for work but with no luck; by now, they had serious financial troubles. Her grandfather had died some months before, and they had to move out of the low-rent apartment he had owned. He evidently had no will, so the property had to be sold to pay off his debts. Leah finally collapsed and was hospitalized for a week. Even as she rested in the hospital, she could not stop worrying about her precious baby.

Finally her husband found work, but one month later the company folded without paying him his last paycheck. Shortly afterward, he had hernia surgery. He was still out of work, but now he didn't have the motivation to even go out and look for a job. The stress shifted to their marriage; they weren't getting along with each other.

As the end of her pregnancy neared, Leah became frightened about labor and delivery. She also worried because she did not want to work after the baby was born, yet she was too scared to quit because of the insecurity of her marriage.

The bright spot came when her happy, healthy baby girl was born. Leah was so proud of her baby and also proud of how she handled herself during labor and delivery. Unfortunately, her moments of joy were cut short because she knew she still had some tough times ahead.

About one week after the baby was born, she sat quietly admiring her beautiful girl as she slept. She loved her so much and was delighted to be her mother. Yet, she was constantly worried about their future and was experiencing inexplicable stomach aches.

One day, however, she was suddenly filled with hope. "Such a wonderful, warm, flooding feeling filled me. I knew that I would do what was best for my baby and everything would work out." She quit work and her lingering stomach aches went away. A month later, her husband had three job offers in one day. "Things weren't easy, not at all, but they kept getting better.

"Now, six years later, I look at my three children and can't help but have hope for the future . . . hope for them . . . hope that I will watch them grow and live out their lives." She felt her first hope many years before and trusts that it will keep coming back any time she needs it.

* * *

Richard's first experience with hope came when he was a young boy just out of high school at what he calls "the ripe old age of nineteen." Because both of his grandfathers were pastors for several churches in his small hometown, Richard was reared "to fear the fire and brimstone, hell and damnation, and God the Almighty!"

His parents had separated when he was young, and his mother was supporting all three children. At the end of high school, he realized he wasn't going anywhere in his hometown so he decided to join the United States Army. "I hoped it would help me to grow up a little bit and maybe help me work toward getting a higher education."

The first step was boot camp, eight "horrible" weeks. He and the other newcomers were constantly screamed at, harassed, and physically and mentally pushed to the point of defeat. "They said it was going to make men out of us," he explains. "I must admit I had my doubts." After those eight grueling weeks, the infantry soldiers-to-be were assigned to Ft. Benning, Georgia, without a break.

On the bus to Georgia they were told horror stories about how infantry training would make boot camp look like kindergarten."They didn't lie!" Richard comments. From the moment they arrived, their lives were a constant struggle. Up at four in the morning and to bed at 11:30 or 12:00 at night, if they were lucky.

One day, they had to complete a twenty-five-mile forced road march in eight hours. Richard says he just wanted to die after returning from the march; he just wanted to give up. His muscles ached, his feet hurt, and he felt like crying. He managed to get into bed. As he lay there feeling as if it were the end of the world, he sensed a breath on his forehead. Startled, he thought that that breath had come from someone who was only an inch away from his forehead. What was even scarier was the fact that he was on the top bunk and very close to the ceiling. He opened his eyes with a jerk and realized that no one was there.

That's when he panicked. "My mind began to think of a million things a second, the first thought being, 'Oh, my God! What was that???' I had no idea; I couldn't explain it." So Richard told himself that it wasn't real because if it was, it would happen again. WHAM!! Just as that thought crossed his mind, he felt it again. Only this moment, the breath was on the very bottom of his throbbing feet underneath the blankets.

This time, however, he wasn't scared because on this occasion a presence in the room made itself known to him. "Truly, it must have been God Himself," Richard says, because he never felt so much love and compassion or joy in all his life. For him, it was "totally indescribable."

The incident truly touched his heart and reached the remote regions of his soul. "It made me believe in invisible forces. It made me believe in God, but most of all it gave me hope. Hope that one day in the future I would be blessed with the opportunity to once again experience God's unconditional love for humanity."

Several years later Richard, still in the U.S. Army, was stationed in the Federal Republic of Germany. It was a day like any other normal day. Nothing really special happened to set this day apart until that night. He went to sleep at about 10:00 p.m. and was sleeping soundly when he was again awakened by a spirit.

This time the spirit was like an old friend. Richard instantly trusted it and was guided from his bed toward the ceiling. As he floated toward the top of the room, he looked down and saw his physical body lying there asleep, completely unaware. The familiar spirit guided him out through the ceiling into the sky above his living quarters.

The two of them began to move quite rapidly across the countryside to places Richard had never seen. It was a marvelous journey during which he was shown the keys to many mysteries that he had always wondered about. For him, it was truly a beautiful world.

After seeing these glorious sights, he was brought back to the countryside near his quarters in Germany. He could see all the familiar homes and, after a short time, sure enough, there were his quarters. They floated right down through the roof and ceiling. And there was his body on the bed sleeping soundly. He sensed it was time to go back to his body, but before he did, he was told that he would not remember what he had seen; he would only remember his trip. At that moment of thought, Richard awoke in his bed looking at the ceiling. He was awed at what had just happened and knew it was real and not just a dream.

Today, twenty years later, Richard cannot recall anything he saw on his journey with the spirit. "But," he writes, "what I learned will be with me when I hit the grave. What did I learn? I learned that I had been on the other side of life—the side that we call death. To me it was as real as the eyes you're reading with. I am no longer afraid of death. I have hope. A hope that will be with me through many more lifetimes, until one day, I can again be aware of the God within. If you've had the opportunity to read this, I think it's because God wanted you to. God Bless Us Everyone!!!"

Richard's story, like the rest of those in this chapter, reminds us that threads of hope weave throughout our lives and beyond. Some small reinforcements of hope can occur earlier in life and can activate later. The daily goal, however, should be to shrink the periods of hopelessness that are bound to slip into the weaving cycle by thinking about an experience that helps you feel hopeful and keeps you going, as did Pearl and the others. Perhaps hope was triggered in your heart by a relative or a teacher from long ago, by a song or by a color. Or perhaps it was spontaneously inspired by God. Recall it again in your mind, and think of the memory as an opportunity you were given to feel your own renewable hope emerge.

✳ ✳ ✳

Phyllis had the opportunity to call upon hope several times over the years because of her son Parker, who had been plagued with difficulties for most of his life. Parker had had severe behaviorial problems from the time he was very young, and she and her son started seeing a counselor when he was only six years old. It took her one-and-a-half years to find a school that would take him. Counseling was not a real help. Through it all, Parker was often given different diagnoses; the most recurrent, however, was hyperactivity with attention deficit disorder, an exhausting challenge for both him and his mother.

The parade of professionals whom she consulted seemed to always assume that Phyllis was the problem. She can't recall how many effective parenting classes she attended, all aimed at teaching her not to break her child's spirit. Yet, at the classes she never learned how to actually help her child.

Finally, in her forties, he attacked her with a baseball bat. Though he didn't hit her, the walls still have several bruises. She called the police and had Parker placed in the custody of children's services—for the third time. For some reason, at this point of defeat, Parker suddenly got better. Phyllis says now, "He is no longer hyperactive. His attention deficit disorder seems to have disappeared, and he is able to sit down and discuss his troublesome problems without 'going off.' "

Phyllis explains that it was her renewing hope which has healed them both. "Right from the beginning, each night when I went to bed, I'd think, 'Tomorrow has to be better.' Each morning, I'd say to myself, 'Maybe today will bring the change.' You see, I always hoped he would outgrow it. I just never knew when."

It was her renewable hope that kept her going from one doctor to another, from one counselor to another, from one argument to another, and from one day to another. She still has an endless supply of hope, but it looks as if she won't be needing it again for awhile.

* * *

Hope has been a strong thread through Brigitte's life. As a then-recently married, twenty-year-old bank teller, she first became aware of the power of hope when her father's fragile health took a turn for the worse. Then her apartment was robbed, and most of what little she had was stolen. By the time she had married, her father had already lived through five heart attacks; now he was seriously ill again. Brigitte's husband didn't work, so they lived in the ghettos of Detroit on her minimum-wage salary. They did not have a phone or a car. All of her income went to rent, utilities, and food. To make matters worse, her life was threatened by local bullies and her husband would do nothing to protect her.

Brigitte became so depressed that she considered suicide. When she wasn't considering suicide, she thought about divorce. She finally decided to go through a divorce instead of taking her own life. Her decision gave her hope for the first time in her life. On the day she made that decision, however, her father died from cancer. Soon, she pulled away from everyone, especially her friends. All she would do from that day on was go to work, then return home.

While going through a period of healing, she met a man named Jessey. He was very considerate compared to her ex-husband. She was beginning to feel hopeful again. Brigitte and Jessey lived together for two years before they were married. Two years later, they became parents of their first and only child, a little girl named Bebee. Although their lives should have been joyous, Bebee seemed to exhibit some unforeseen emotional problems. Somewhere deep in her heart, however, Brigitte was still very unhappy.

When Bebee started first grade, she developed an ulcer. After she was tested by medical doctors and a psychologist, it was discovered that little Bebee was gifted; however, a portion of her brain's frontal lobe had not finished developing. It was this unfinished frontal lobe that was causing her to have constant temper tantrums.

Brigitte took Bebee back to the psychologist to help her daughter get control of her own emotions. She also moved her to a new school, hoping it would cure her ulcers. Fortunately it worked, and again Brigitte took hope from a decision she had made. Bebee was getting better, but by now Brigitte and Jessey had begun to have marital troubles. They were struggling through marriage counseling with no progress in sight.

With her daughter finally doing well, it was Brigitte's turn to find out why she was still so unhappy. She asked her daughter's doctor if he would also treat her. The trusted psychologist asked Brigitte to write about her marriage and to describe her husband's good and bad points. When he reviewed her list, he agreed that, despite what she thought, she really did not have a good marriage. He did promise, however, to help her find ways to cope if she loved her husband and wanted to stay in the marriage.

After some soul-searching and simultaneously recovering from an operation to try to restore the hearing in her left ear, Brigitte made a decision: she did not love her husband after all. She didn't need any more help from the psychologist because her decision had again triggered her renewable hope. She could continue her journey of achieving happiness without professional help.

With no job or degree, she enrolled in a bachelor's program in accounting. She decided to divorce her second husband of twelve years. Through all these complicated and emotional changes, her hope had returned and she soon believed that she and her daughter would be all right. She explains that they have been fine since and that counting on recurrent hope has become her new pattern for living.

Around the time that she completed the A.R.E. research project questionnaire, Brigitte made the decision to go on to graduate school. She was planning to move with her daughter to a new city where the graduate school was located. Since her father's death over a decade ago, Brigitte had no family to assist her. Jessey, though supportive financially, never visited Bebee, so she expects the move to be a clean and easy one.

Now, she relates, when she gets frightened about making yet another major life change, she feels her hope kicking in and quickly remembers that everything will work out. "So far, I trust in God or the spirit within, and I have the recurring experience of hope. My life has been O.K. We have never starved, and our necessities in life have been taken care of. Jobs have always presented themselves when money has gotten low, and friends have been available when I needed companionship."

She has not become romantically involved with anyone since the divorce. From time to time she feels lonely, however, and would like to have another adult with whom to share her life. "I believe that if I am patient," she writes, "the right man will enter my life. If I did not have hope, then I don't think life would be worth living."

Brigitte has the gift of renewable hope. She had hope in the past that set her free from two bad marriages. She had hope that convinced her to try to attend college, and now her hope is again traveling with her to a new city and through a tough graduate program. She has enough hope to last her a lifetime, and the way she's growing and changing, her hope will be very busy indeed.

✳ ✳ ✳

We can all access renewable hope. In fact, you may already have it and not realize it. It needs only to be recalled by a scent, a vision, a sound, or a thought. Close your eyes and think back to a time when you felt hope. Perhaps the feeling came from a relative, like Pearl's Aunt Meg. Perhaps it came from a decision you made, as it has many times in Brigitte's life; or from a vision, as happened to Richard. When you are faced with a conflict, a tragedy, or a sudden fear, carefully consider the situations in your life that have made you feel happy, peaceful, and sure of yourself, and soon your old hope will be remembered, restored, and re-lived.

12
HOPE
IS STRONG

"Great are your abilities.
Great are your hopes.
So, too, great are your
responsibilities! For those to
whom much is given is much required."

Based on Edgar Cayce Reading 262-121

Strong hope does for our spirits what adrenaline does for runners, prize fighters, or soldiers dodging bullets. Like adrenaline, strong hope is used to quell our biggest fears and to rescue us from our toughest trials. Only strong hope is tough enough to wrestle down our deepest anxiety, to steer us through our worst depression, and to lift us out of danger. This kind of hope is available to all of us, but only for our most serious tasks.

* * *

Fourteen years ago a young man named Harry, in air force basic training in San Antonio, Texas, experienced first-hand the hope that gives us strength. In the hard-nosed world of the military, his hope arrived to out-muscle the macho mentality that surrounded him. Harry's division had marched into a field for a special awards ceremony for an elite group of officers. The squad leader ordered Harry and his comrades to stand in formation and wait for the general who was late. The heat of the day beat down on the airmen as they waited at parade rest, their legs apart and their hands behind their backs.

As the thick 102-degree air began to weaken their concentration, the squad leader told them to bend their knees to keep the circulation going in their lower legs. Harry heard an order given: if the airman in front of you falls, remain at parade rest, and let that person fall. The squad leader said he would remove the fallen airman from the formation.

As the wait wore on, people started falling around Harry. In the next line, a young female recruit fell to the ground as the airman directly behind her watched, unable to help. Her head hit the ground like a stone, and she lay unconscious until the squad leader pulled her out of formation. Harry had been sweating steadily. He was terrified that he would be the next to drop. As he stood with his knees bent in the Texas heat, he began to feel the presence of his Uncle Leonard, who had passed away four years earlier.

Suddenly Harry felt himself inside a circle of light with this uncle. The heavy air was blown out of the circle, and it felt cool and refreshing. His uncle's voice reminded Harry of two photographs back home in the living room—one of Leonard and one of Harry's father when they were each in the army during World War II. Leonard's soothing voice explained that they also had experienced basic training and had survived this kind of discipline.

His uncle's presence pumped him with confidence and helped him to understand that this kind of experience was essential to his development. For the first time, Harry states,

"I began to see that our strength is always being tested in this world and that I was strong enough to endure."

As he looked around, he noticed that there were other formations of light around the group, encircling the fallen airmen. Harry could feel the strength of hope penetrating his whole squad. When the ceremony ended, he grappled with the humidity once more. Yet, as he marched through the sticky air back to the barracks, he didn't feel the temperature; he was instead feeling that he would never again be alone in his life's trials. His new hope held the blistering heat at bay and showed him a way to survive his discomfort.

Harry secretly promised himself that when he went back home to Michigan, he would contact his Aunt Jane and tell her about the experience with Uncle Leonard. Four years passed before Harry told anyone what had happened that hot day in San Antonio. Finally he told his father and asked to be taken to Aunt Jane's trailer. His father was negative, almost frightened by the story of the circle of light and the vision of his late brother. He asked Harry not to visit Jane—not to take the story any further.

Although Harry didn't understand, he accepted his father's wishes and didn't contact his aunt. He just hoped the time would come when he could do so. Two years later, after his father died, Harry contacted Aunt Jane. She had not heard from any of the family since Leonard's death. This was Harry's chance to tell her the whole story of the strength he had received from her late husband. She was neither frightened nor surprised. She said quietly, "He loved you very much." Harry replied, "I know, and he was my favorite uncle."

* * *

Sometimes we need more than a single, strong shot of

hope. Sometimes we need the long-distance enduring kind of hope that will give us the strength of a marathon runner. In 1968, Morris was a graduate student in economics at Iowa State University. He had been married for nine years to a strong, patient woman named Ann Marie and they had a six-year-old daughter. At the time he had been in such a long, deep depression that he was physically unable to smile.

One day, as he labored over a draft of his Ph.D. dissertation, he realized he had written the same sentence over and over again "at least a thousand times." The next morning he kissed Ann Marie and daughter Maggy good-by, took his car about five miles out of town, and intentionally drove into a concrete bridge abutment at sixty-five miles an hour, without a seat belt. When he awoke in intensive care, he had tubes in his throat and a cast on his right ankle. He was in traction for a shattered thigh bone, his nose and right jaw had been pulverized, his teeth were wired shut, his left knee was shattered, and he had five broken ribs. He had been on the operating table for ten-and-one-half hours. His wife had been told by the doctors that he was as good as dead.

When they learned that his accident had really been a suicide attempt, the doctors put Morris on anti-depressants. The shock of the accident, however, had jolted him out of his depression, and the drugs sent him into a euphoric high. Early one morning in the hospital he had a startling vision in "brilliant technicolor." He was at the Last Supper, and Jesus washed his feet and dried them with His hair. This powerful vision gave Morris hope for the first time in his life.

For him, this vision was just the beginning, for it would take an extended dose of strong hope to maintain this newly found high following his removal from the drug. In order to defend himself against his own despair, he would have to keep hope alive in his head and heart for the next two decades. Even though Morris's wife had always been steadfast in her support of him— and her love was uncompromising—it was the vision of Jesus washing his feet that led him to begin to believe he was a worthy person. Slowly he began to realize he had nothing of which to be ashamed. "That experience gave me a strong and enduring hope to find a fulfilling new life."

In retrospect, Morris sees that it was hope that had given him the strength to triumph. When the doctors said he would die, he lived. When the doctors told him he would never walk again, he walked. Then the doctors told him he would have a significant limp and have to use a cane; today he walks without a cane. The doctors also told him that his right leg would be one or two inches shorter than his left. Morris's legs, after his hospitalization, are exactly the same length. One doctor told him his nose would surely collapse when the swelling went down because of all the broken bones. In three weeks the doctor returned, looked at Morris's nose which had healed normally, and gasped, "That's impossible!" It seems that his hope for living a new life was too strong to be defeated.

Before the accident, Morris had worn a cross around his neck, always hidden from sight. Since the accident, he now makes sure the cross is always in view. Before his accident, he had the love of his wife, but that love hadn't seemed strong enough for him. Now he believes in God because, he explains, "My mind was slammed into awareness when my body was slammed into the concrete wall. God helped me come back from that."

Over twenty years later, sitting in his rocking chair in his living room in Minnesota and listening to jazz, Morris reflected: "In the last twenty-three years I have played tennis—in tournaments and for recreation. For twenty-one years I have been a college professor. I have raised two lovely and unique daughters. I know many wonderful and competent students, and I have found such a multitude of miracles in my life that they seem uncountable."

Morris also describes his life as one that has known trouble, illness, pain, separation, and misery. But equally he has experienced joy, rewarding accomplishments, and valuable experiences. He playfully concludes, "If there isn't hope in my story for someone out there, then I'm a monkey's uncle . . . which I probably am."

* * *

Trent tells of another way in which hope can give strength. His hope emerged like the bursting speed of a sprinter, just strong enough and just long enough. The last week in October 1989 was the worst week of Trent's life. On Wednesday he found out that his father, who had undergone a successful operation for stomach cancer the previous year, was facing a recurrence of his disease. This time it was inoperable. Trent didn't have to ask: he knew it would be terminal. Chemotherapy was the only method to try to extend his father's life.

On Friday of that week, Trent's boss called him into his office and told him that the financial conditions at his company were such that he had to be laid off from his position in air pollution control research. Although his wife worked, he had no hope for his situation. He felt only sorrow and fear. Trent knew he would have to break the news of his unemployment to his father and that made the layoff even worse. His father, already depressed about his own condition, did not take his son's news well. He, too, was without hope.

The following Monday Trent began to think about working in a different industry; perhaps a university or the state's Department of Environmental Protection (DEP) would have an opening. A week later, after numerous tries, he finally got through to the chairperson of the environmental department of the state university in his hometown, who suggested that Trent call a man named Bill Dawson at the state DEP. Suddenly, at that suggestion, Trent could feel hope flexing its muscles.

He called Bill Dawson who told him there was a hiring freeze; however, he was interested in Trent and suggested that he send him a résumé and call him periodically in case there were any changes. Hope was getting stronger. He told his father, and his father's spirits improved—Trent's story was just the right tonic of hope for his father.

For the next eight months he kept looking for jobs and going to a number of interviews, but with no results. He did, however, continue to call the state DEP. Trent's father had been responding well enough to the chemotherapy treatments to maintain a near-normal life, but his condition was not to last. He became weaker and finally was hospitalized.

That summer, the DEP called Trent for an interview. A week later the department offered him a job. He visited his father in the hospital that night and told him the good news that he would be starting work in two weeks. During his first week of work his father peacefully passed over.

It took some time for Trent, now forty, to realize just how hope had figured into those months of turmoil. "In retrospect, although hope was important to me, it was the strength and power of hope that kept my father alive during that difficult time in my life."

* * *

The strength and power of hope is also evidenced in Irene's story. She was only fourteen years old in 1945, and she was in Germany—struggling along with the rest of the country through the last horrible days of WWII. She and her family had been on the road for eight days as refugees from

East Germany. Having to leave a homesite that had been the property of the family for over 700 years was traumatic, but leaving it under the guns of Russian tanks was a tragedy for them all.

One particular day they found themselves under fire from Russian airplanes for hours. Most of the time they spent lying face down in a shallow ditch, while shells flew around them. They finally were able to ferry across the frigid Elbe River with two military trucks full of ammunition. The airplanes continued their attacks for the entire forty-five minutes it took to cross.

As Irene crouched under one of the trucks, she was fully aware that it could blow up at any moment. Yet she felt totally safe, totally protected, and—in spite of everything that was going on in her war-torn world—she felt hope. Though she had no idea where that strong hope came from, nevertheless, she simply trusted it.

"That experience, deep inside me and unshared by the rest of my family, has continued to carry me through. From that day on there was always that knowing that I would live, that I had a purpose, and that there was something mightier than myself offering powerful hope. This feeling of hope and trust has served me well over the years, especially now as I am going through difficult times—it is with me."

In her sixties, Irene now reflects on how hope has continued to give her strength in her life, ever since that day on the ferry. Her husband has had Parkinson's disease since a year after they were married in 1979. She works as a massage therapist and has provided for his home care since the beginning, though she barely remembers the person she once married and the love that they had known.

Yet, she says, "I do all to the best of my ability. The hope and trust that all is well does carry me—most of the time. Without it, I would have bailed out of this situation many years ago."

❋ ❋ ❋

Hope is available to us in varying degrees of strength. We have the big heavy hope to combat our equally heavy problems, and we have the quick jabbing hope like the swift punch of a prize fighter to knock the wind out of our despair. We have only to reach inside for the kind of hope we need. From the extended, supportive kind to the sudden, quick bursts, hope is tough enough for any challenge.

Think for a moment about your own experience with the strong side of hope. Remember a time when your hope had to be tougher than your fears and doubts. You probably didn't recognize it then, but there was a time in your life when hope literally bullied its way in and outlasted your problems. From your own memories, as well as from the stories of Harry and Morris and the others, you'll now be able to identify strong hope when it appears.

13
HOPE
IS SURPRISING

*"Hope is that thing
with feathers
That perches in the soul..."*

Emily Dickenson

Sometimes hope arrives when you least expect it, when you're stuck in a melancholy mood or trapped with a bad attitude. With little warning it can sneak up behind you and startle you into another thought pattern or a new direction. And it almost always inspires you with the one solution you had never imagined. Its effect is to rattle and remind you that anything can happen and that everything is possible. Like the other sides of hope, surprising hope has different levels of intensity. For example, someone who is deeply in thought needs only a quick, slick surprise to change his or her mood, whereas another in deep depression may need an out-of-the-blue blast to change his or her world.

✳ ✳ ✳

A teacher in the Chicago public school system, Ann was bushwacked by the surprising side of hope. Every day on her way to the lunchroom she is lost in thoughts, usually preoccupied about some problem from the morning. And every day the same petite and plain-looking young girl says hello to her.

Ann has worked for the public schools for a long time. She knows that a lot of kids think she looks mean and that several of her former students are afraid of her. Even if she is in a great mood, she keeps a serious look on her face. In her line of work, that's probably not a bad idea. Consequently, her stern mask has become a habit, so she is always a little surprised when this former student says hello to her in such a cheerful, open manner. Although Ann does recognize this student, the young girl is so unremarkable that Ann barely remembers her being in class. This year, however, they both have lunch at the same time, so Ann sees her every day.

Recently, when Ann was walking through the lunchroom with another teacher, the young girl approached her with her daily smile and happily said, "Hello." The other teacher commented on how sweet and sincere the girl was. Then she asked Ann the girl's name. Ann was stunned to realize that she didn't know.

For the rest of the day she thought about this nameless young girl, but she couldn't remember much about her except that she had been her student. "No matter what kind of a foul mood I'm in, when I walk into that lunchroom, she cheers me up with her kind words and friendly smile. She's like a guardian angel, there to remind me on a daily basis that I don't have to be so negative and angry-looking all the time."

For the next several days the girl was absent, and Ann really missed her. When she finally saw her back in the lunchroom, Ann forgot her defensive face. Smiling, she rushed right up to her and told her what a good example she was and how thoughtful of her to always say hello. Then Ann pretended that she had only momentarily forgotten the girl's name saying, "I don't know what's wrong with me today, for some reason I just can't think of your name!" With a smile that lit up the whole room, the young girl said, "I'm Hope!"

✳ ✳ ✳

As you can see, there is no way to prepare for surprising hope. When we least expect it, it jumps up and says "Boo" to any area of our life, love, work, or play. Like Ann, this next woman had no warning of the brief, but beautiful, awakening of her own surprising hope.

At thirty-six years of age, Rianna was moving. She wasn't moving to marry someone or to find someone new, but in order to quiet the little voice inside of her that said, "Keep going. Keep moving. Keep growing." She had made the difficult decision to quit her sales job in southern California and seek a new direction. Although she did have faith in her decision, she was still scared, alone, and unsure of herself. After living on the West Coast for almost twenty years, Rianna, her heart filled with fear and her eyes glowing with adventure, embarked on a move across country to the East Coast.

She had decided to take some extra time along the way. After all, she had no job to go to and no one waiting for her at the other end of her journey. By the second week of her trip, as she was winding her little car through the mighty Yosemite National Park on her way to Kings Canyon in southeast California, Rianna realized it was February 14, Valentine's Day.

Self-pity started to pick at her. She was alone, had no

company, and no one with whom to share this adventure. The sun was shrinking, the night sky was growing over the trees and mountains, and suddenly she realized she was all by herself in the middle of nowhere. She was tired and hungry. The road ahead looked bleak, so she decided to turn around and go to a hotel she had seen about twenty miles back.

As she pulled off the road to make a U-turn, the little voice inside of her said, "Keep going forward." She shouted, "No, no, there's nothing ahead." But the voice kept insisting and finally Rianna got back on the road and reluctantly headed into the darkness. She had traveled only ten miles when she came to a tiny, cozy restaurant that seemed to be carefully perched on the side of the road. Relieved, she quickly stopped to eat—reminding herself to ask about the closest place to stay for the night.

When she walked in, she was greeted by the owner who handed her a beautiful long-stemmed red rose and wished her a Happy Valentine's Day. She was so astounded that she just stood there. Slowly she began feeling the warmth of the room embrace her as she turned the stem in her trembling hand. When she finally recovered, she sat down and ordered a nourishing meal. Before she could slip back into her feeling of aloneness again, the waitress placed a free glass of champagne at her table, then included her in a lively conversation with the owner and other customers. She felt truly blessed and was filled with hope for a successful journey.

With a full stomach and happy heart, Rianna's body began to remember the miles she had just driven. Her back began to ache and her eyes felt dry and dusty. It was time to move on — to find a place to stay for the night. She asked for directions and was totally amazed to hear that there were cabins for rent right behind the restaurant for only $25.00 a night. This wonderful news made her laugh right out loud. What a surprising way to end an out-of-the-ordinary evening.

For Rianna, surprising hope arrived like a splash of water, catching her breath and changing her mood. First came the shock of the rose—something that she had never expected or imagined. Jolted out of her loneliness, she was actually too surprised to even smile, so she just stood there with her fresh flower. Then, ever so slowly, she began to feel a fresh rebirth of hope—for her trip, for her decision, and for herself.

Another splash of surprising hope came when she discovered that there was a place for her to sleep right beyond the restaurant's back door. This kind of surprise, on the heels of being handed a rose, made her laugh out loud, shake her head, and say to herself, "This is more than I even hoped for."

The red rose? It lived for the rest of the trip, all the way to the East Coast. When Rianna got to Virginia and parked her car, she looked down at the still-vibrant flower on her front seat, smiled, nodded her head, and said, "Yes. This is where I should be."

* * *

For some, hope emerges only at the end of a journey—after a long stretch of sadness or pain or fear. For Grace, surprising hope arrived just in the nick of time or, as she says, "Hope came *with* the last straw." In 1978, only weeks after finding out that she was pregnant with her second child, Grace also discovered that her husband had fallen in love with someone else—and that someone else was a man. Not only was her husband, Ross, in love with this other man, but he had also made a commitment to him. Consequently, Ross, a professional dancer, began a life separate from Grace and became emotionally and physically distant from her from that point on.

While absorbing this devastating news of her husband

having a male lover, Grace was caught off guard by the opportunity to shift her career and change her job to what she describes as a more interesting path. Without any thought, she accepted the offer even though it meant sacrificing her existing medical coverage for the pregnancy and delivery. As the days dragged by, Ross's dance company began to fall apart. By early 1979, the dancers were asked to continue working without pay in the hopes that one more gala performance would save the company.

Four months later, Grace gave birth to a dark-eyed baby girl whom she named Melissa, and she began her maternity leave without pay. That same week Ross's dance company closed without paying the dancers for their months of work. The small savings she had was already gone so she borrowed money from friends for rent and food.

Two weeks after returning to work, Grace got her first paycheck only to turn around and spend half of it for baby sitters. Ross didn't help with money or child care. He couldn't find work in Cleveland because most of the dance companies in that area had fallen on hard times. So Grace was truly alone with the family responsibilities. It was summer before Ross finally got a real job offer, but it was for a dance company in Europe. Since nothing else had opened up for him in all these months, he and his lover decided to go.

After Grace had dropped off her husband and his lover at the airport on that hot, heavy August night, she finally hit bottom. She had to face the fact that her marriage was over. As all that reality started to sink in, she became overwhelmed with the prospect of single parenting two children and facing her debts alone. She wept until the morning.

The next day, the consulting firm she worked for lost a large contract with the federal government, and Grace was out of a job. The company's headquarters were on the other side of the state, so a transfer for her and the children was out of the question. Her boss was very concerned about her as she sat in front of him during her closing interview. Amazingly though, after living through the most frightening year of her life and now on the edge of losing her livelihood, Grace suddenly felt the most startling, unlikely "incredibly surprising surge of hope pulsing through my body."

She was flabbergasted that this apparently hopeless situation didn't crush her—it actually energized her. Rather than falling apart, she surprised herself by consoling her boss. Shocked, she heard her own voice telling him that this news really meant a new beginning, that it was the best she could have gotten. It was ridiculous to feel hope now—at a time like this—yet she did.

After her boss recovered from his own surprise at her response, he called his friend at a recruiting agency. By the end of the day, Grace had gathered her résumé and some notes and was on her way to an intake interview with the recruiter. She ought to have been the most desperate job seeker on the planet, but instead, in awe, she heard herself describing her dream job to the recruiter. She quoted him a salary of twenty-five percent more than she had been making and told him that she would take a job only in her suburb of Cleveland because of her children.

The recruiter, who seemed surprised at her requirements, arranged two interviews for her the next day. The first was only a mile from her home in a new office building, right next to a grocery store—a very important location for a single mom. Grace interviewed with the publications manager of the firm and liked him right away. The job he needed to fill was exactly what she wanted. Before she left the interview, he offered her the job at more than she had asked.

That surprising surge of hope that had happened so

many years ago catapulted Grace into some very positive and rewarding changes in her life. In her new job she was encouraged to be creative, which resulted in several award-winning publications. She met many bright and exciting people, one of whom she believed to be her soul mate. He became her second husband and the father of her son. Within four years, Grace became the publications manager. If she had not been faced with those surprising challenges, she would never have needed to call upon her own supply of hope—but worse—she would not have had such a delightful ending to her story.

＊　＊　＊

Surprising hope had served its purpose in Grace's life very well. Now the same kind of hope was about to be discovered by another single mom named Arlene, living in Washington state. Arlene didn't need a super surge of hope, but was about to receive a very surprising hug. After fourteen years of marriage and a thirteen-year-old son, she suddenly found herself single. Her husband moved out one night without warning. The thought of wanting or needing another relationship scared her so she buried herself in a quest to complete her four-year degree in accounting.

Within two years, Arlene's husband officially became engaged to another woman; thus, it was time to face squarely her future and file for divorce. The finality of the divorce tossed her into a deep and monotonous depression. She didn't realize it at first because she had kept herself so busy working and going to school. But when she took off one school term, she realized that she had lost touch with herself while burying her feelings beneath a busy schedule.

Having been a student of the Edgar Cayce readings since 1974, she not so coincidentally one day attended a psychic fair near her home. The afternoon at the fair led to some hypnotic personality regression work and on to resolving some old pain and conflict. Arlene also began to re-read some books based on Cayce's work, to review her prayers, and re-experience meditation. One quiet, calm afternoon she had a clear vision along with a feeling of genuine love and warmth coming her way. She saw herself sitting on her sofa with warm arms around her.

A few months later, Todd, her son, told her about a man who lived in their mobile home park. He described him as a really nice man with a good sense of humor. He pestered his mother until she finally met him one day on a walk in the park. The two talked and instantly enjoyed each other's energy. For two weeks they dated—dinner, dancing, and movies. One night they decided to spend some time at Arlene's and watch some TV. Arlene says that, much to her surprise, "We sat on the sofa and a little while later those warm arms were holding me, and my vision of hope was realized."

✳ ✳ ✳

Hope arrived unexpectedly for Noreen when she was very young—only eleven years old. But that hope has stayed with her for the last fifty years. She recalls that many years ago, on her last day of sixth grade, she had a terrible fight with her best friend. Their angry words ended with a promise to never have anything to do with each other ever again. They didn't see or speak to one another for the whole summer—a lifetime to an eleven-year-old.

September arrived, and Noreen was faced with seeing her estranged friend, Martha. She had thought about her relationships all summer long and decided that she wanted to be Martha's best friend again. On the night before the first day of school, Noreen prayed and asked for God's advice. Suddenly the room was filled with the brightest light she had ever seen. "Its warmth penetrated into every corner and enveloped me with peace and love. It withdrew as quickly as it had arrived, and soon I was off in a blissful sleep."

She awoke the next morning feeling confident, knowing she could face whatever Martha felt for her—anger, silence, even a rebuff. When Noreen got to school, Martha was already on the playground and came running up to her, gave her a big hug, and told her how much she had missed her over the summer. Astounded, Noreen just stood there, completely taken aback. This was not the emotion she had expected. She reminded her friend of the nasty fight they had had just before their vacation. Martha looked bewildered for a moment and said, "I don't remember any fight."

It took some time before Noreen realized that the incident had lingered only in her own mind. Obviously Martha had not given it another thought. Once she recovered from the surprise, Noreen caught up with Martha's attitude of it being over and done with; with new hope the young girls became best friends again.

Having had many ups and downs since that surprising September morning, Noreen says, "I was one of the lucky ones. A beautiful, bright, forgiving hope was revealed to me when I was eleven years old. I have prayed to hope, meditated on it, and invoked many blessings since then." But she has learned that surprising hope makes itself known in its own time and its own way. Not knowing when it will arrive doesn't spoil its power. That is what makes it a surprise.

The only way of welcoming surprising hope into your life is by not expecting it. Surprising hope will always provide you with the solution that you never ever expected. Instead of trying to arrange an experience with the surprising side of hope, just prepare yourself by staying open. Open your heart, open your eyes, and open your thoughts to the unusual. Sure enough, the unexpected will pop up, change your mind, and change your mood.

14
HOPE
IS VAST

*"Hope is that calling
heard within, to push us on to greater
awareness, to pull up the fences of limitations, and
to expand to include today's miracles as tomorrow's
common everyday experiences."*

Nancy Rajala of Cedarburg, Wisconsin
Editor of *The Inner Voice*

I f we give it a chance, hope can put everything into perspective for us. It reminds us that we are indeed the smaller parts of the vast great plan. Vast hope offers mountains of encouragement, oceans of promise, and a sky full of reasons to keep on trying.

* * *

Maya grew up in India. Even as a young girl, she felt a great sense of injustice for the way women were treated in her homeland. Early in her life she had decided she would escape. Perhaps to America. But how? How could she leave her male-ruled country when she couldn't even leave her house without a chaperone. In her culture, even to get into college, Maya would have to have her father's signature on the application because she was a single female.

Because of American immigration quotas, however, Maya discovered that there was a twenty-year waiting period. Her older sisters were quickly being married off and soon it would be her turn. There seemed to be no way out of India and no way out of an arranged marriage, arranged future, and an arranged life.

One day, without permission and without chaperones, Maya decided to make the long journey to the seaside. She needed the openness of the ocean. She needed to look at herself against the backdrop of an endless body of water. In the still morning hours she sneaked to the railway station and took the train to Bombay, about 100 miles from her home village. From the sooty city of Bombay, she took a bus to the ocean. All alone, she started walking at the ocean's edge, talking to God, asking how she would ever leave India with her freedom intact.

Within moments, a wild storm arose. Huge sheets of water were smashing wet and noisy on the coastline. But instead of being afraid, Maya was drenched in joy! She screamed with the thunder and danced with the rain and let the ocean waves pour over her. In a few minutes, this rare out-of-season storm had passed, and the waves went back to their rhythmic rolling. She called it her storm of hope. After the storm Maya was full of unshakable confidence and knew that in spite of the twenty-year waiting period for emigration to the U.S., she would get out in good time. The massive storm triggered her hope that she would be free.

About four years after her storm-of-hope experience, when she was twenty years old, her father finally agreed to help her get to Hong Kong. Undaunted, from there she got permission to go to Canada. "I nearly froze in Montreal, and in 1967 I was finally able to move to California where my only American friend lived."

Maya quickly filed papers for citizenship. She was so convinced that this was the country where she belonged that she argued with the immigration department for seven years, insisting that she needed no American sponsor to whom she would be obliged. In 1974, just over ten years from her first experience with vast hope, she got her formal immigration card and her U.S. citizenship.

Maya enjoyed being an American woman. Coming and going as she pleased, she traveled the country and made the most of her hard-earned freedom for another fifteen years. In October of 1989, however, it appeared that she had reached a dead end in all her activities and for another year searched for a deeper way to live and a better way to earn a living. What kept coming up for her was that she should start a nonprofit organization to operate group homes for the elderly.

One morning she simply decided to take the day off from everything and stay home. Around 5:00 p.m. the ground started to shake and the windows began to rattle. At first, she thought it was just another one of those California "rollers." However, this one promised to be more. When she realized that the shaking was not going to stop, she headed for the front door. The ground shook again, this time hard enough to jar some pictures from their hooks on the walls and down onto the floor.

The shaking and noise got worse. Cabinets started popping open, and everything began falling out onto the floor. Maya kept moving toward the front door when suddenly she felt as though an enormous hand pushed her into a sitting position on the two steps leading to her entryway. She started to get up, but a large can fell with great force on her arm. She sat back down.

The solid wooden hutch by the front door jumped forward and fell with such force that the cabinet doors were smashed and all the contents were shattered. Maya would have been under that hutch if she had not been forced to sit down only a few seconds before. As she watched her furniture tip over and crack and her lamps smash to the floor, she realized with awe that she had been made to sit in the only safe spot in the house. To any place else that she might have retreated something would have fallen on her! Could this be another storm of hope?

Finally, the earth became still again, and it was safe to venture outdoors to check for structural damage. Other neighbors were cautiously leaving their homes and searching wildly up and down the street. By comparing notes with her bewildered neighbors, Maya discovered that of all the houses on the hill where she lived, her house survived the best. Like all the other residents of the California coast, she went back to her life a little shaken from the earth's gigantic grumbling but soon forgot its impact. She mopped and swept the floors and pieced together what she could, throwing out what she couldn't fix.

Then one day, she was suddenly struck with the thought that for over a year she had been trying to start her own non-profit organization. She realized, too, that just before the quake she had discovered that the initial funds she was going to need to get started were far beyond the sum she could raise. She remembered that on the day of the quake, she had been wondering what her next step would be. "During the quake I had been held back from harm. I knew that surely this was another 'storm of hope' for my behalf." She also knew because she was instantly filled with hope that she somehow had important work to do and would soon know what it was.

Out of curiosity (she thought) she began to read Noel Langley's book *Edgar Cayce on Reincarnation*. She recalls that Cayce said that if you can't do the work you are planning to do, do the nearest thing to it that you can. She thought and thought and remembered that while exploring the group homes idea, she had kept getting involved one way or another with child care. It seemed to her that the laws and regulations were similar. Finally, her answer arrived! She would enter the child-care field.

She tried to get an operating license to care for six children. The county license issuer, who was reputed to be unreasonably tough about approving licenses, persuaded her to ask for a license for twelve children and waived the two-year required waiting period. So she could start right away. Maya had again shortened the waiting period to get where she wanted to be and knew then that child care was the right avenue for her to follow.

At forty-five years of age, she has become well established in child care and is also taking classes for a management certificate for nonprofit organizations. In addition she is trying to start a separate nonprofit day-care center for children who need relief from abusive or potentially abusive situations and families. For Maya, the two major decisions in her life had been inspired by magnificent natural forces. Instead of being afraid, however, both experiences have awakened a great hope in her—a hope that was big enough to help her go after what she wanted in spite of all the obstacles.

* * *

It doesn't always take an earthquake to awaken someone's own supply of vast hope. Sometimes a massive dose of hope that is spread out over a span of time is what is needed to convince us that we can get to where we want to go—if we have hope.

Gail was reared in a hard-working little town on the border between New York and Pennsylvania. The summer when she turned twenty was very exciting for her. She learned to drive a stick-shift car and was getting ready to go back to college in southern New York state, where she was living with her new husband. That autumn, after coming home from a practice drive with the stick-shift, she walked across some wet grass to get a newspaper in front of their apartment building. In what seemed like the slow motion of her mind, she fell and completely dislocated her left ankle.

Fortunately it was mid-afternoon and several people came running over. They called an ambulance. The doctors told her later that a fifteen-minute delay would have meant the loss of her foot. Gail spent eight weeks in the hospital, flat on her back in a full-leg cast. Just before her accident she had been reading *Seth Speaks* and other works by Jane Roberts. Something about those books helped her to mentally review her ankle accident—to remember more than the fall. Thinking later about Roberts' concept of "consciously created circumstances" and "actions reflecting beliefs," Gail was able to ask herself, "Why did I have this happen to me?"

In time she became painfully aware of her subconscious beliefs of low self-esteem, of not really being happy with her relationship or her environment, and her feelings that her life was moving too fast and without introspection. At that point she vowed to believe in her future, to overcome this problem, and to hope for a full recovery. She would need an extended stay from the vast side of hope to meet her physical and emotional challenges.

She spent the next year and a half in three different casts. One of the bones in her foot had a hole which did not want to heal. She continued to read and think and meditate. She recalls the day the last cast was finally removed and how painful it was just to stand on that unused leg. Simultaneously, Gail went through painful physical therapy, all the while walking with a cane. In the end, the doctors told her she had limited range of motion in her anguished ankle and that she would never be able to walk without a limp.

In 1972, Gail contacted Jane Roberts. Cane in hand, she started attending Jane's Tuesday night weekly Psychic Seminars in Elmira, N.Y. Gail lived only fifty miles away at the time and didn't realize until much later that this may have been one reason why she had relocated—it wasn't just for a formal education.

She attended Jane's seminars until 1975. She held out a huge hope that she would walk again without a cane. "I practiced hundreds of visualizations and immeasurable meditations and did group dreams as part of the classes. At the same time, I ignored the doctor's advice and filled up my free time with skiing and ballroom dancing."

As if her life weren't involved or intense enough, there was trouble ahead for her husband Roy. One Tuesday evening during her psychic class, Roy had gone to the library. He was reaching to collect his books from his car which was parked in front of the same apartment building, not ten feet from where Gail had dislocated her ankle. Traveling at great speed, a hit-and-run driver sideswiped the car, crashing into Roy and ripping off the driver's door. Roy was rushed to the hospital. Their landlady saw the whole accident and later told them that he had been thrown into the air and carried about twenty-five feet.

During class, Gail had had a feeling that there was a problem in connection with Roy, but she was not prepared for the magnitude of the accident. She was told about the hit and run and immediately headed for the hospital. Roy was in a coma when she arrived, and this opportunity marked the beginning of a major challenge for Gail. She knew that since he was in a coma, he was deciding whether or not to continue living in this plane. It would take him three more months to decide, and Gail would need the biggest kind of hope to get through this one.

With hope by her side, she sat in their living room with the lights dimmed and mentally asked Roy over and over again to "talk" to her. She slowly began to see a transparent image of Roy fill the easy chair that he loved. He looked semi-solid with hands on the chair arms and feet together, but his eyes were closed and his head was slightly bent forward. Once this image was achieved, she started talking directly to him. A mental communication came back to her, a telepathic answering of her questions, responding to her thoughts. She felt that he seemed bent on indifference to life, to depression, with very stubborn "Why should I live?" thoughts.

With great concentration, Gail focused on answering those questions by listing positive things about the future. She kept asking him to wake up and come back to earth. Her faith was broad and wide and included his recovery. She explains, "Of course, it would work. After all, I still had the enormous hope of creating my own recovery." One day at the hospital, as she sat there softly calling his name, she saw one of his eyes twitch. She excitedly told the nurses, and soon Roy did come out of his coma.

It has been many years since that day that Roy "woke up" in the hospital. Several years after his recovery, the two amicably divorced. Gail is remarried now to a man named Jack whom she met while ballroom dancing. Recently, she and her new husband have opened a ballroom dance studio together. Despite what the doctors told her many years ago, her immense hope is still intact. Gail's accident triggered her hope and got her not only walking again, but dancing. The same vast hope pulled Roy back to this life, and he has since recovered. Her hope has proved vast enough for all her challenges. "I have only a faint limp now when I'm extremely tired or when I am suffering through occasional rainy/snowy weather . . . I live my adult life in and with hope."

* * *

Unlike Gail's, Carol's hopelessness was caused by a global event, and it took a resurgence of vast hope to set her straight. Like most of us, she was emotionally upset and worried by the news of Operation Desert Storm. She was sixty when the first scud missiles slit open the sky over Iraq. She'd already seen too many wars, lost friends and lovers, and now another war. How could this be? On the second morning after U.S. President Bush's announcement, she closed her eyes in meditation, hopeless and sad at the news of another war.

Soon, in her mind's eye a white dove appeared. She tried to ignore it, but it would not go away. She finally relaxed and watched. It flew to a wooden fence, landed there, and picked up in its beak a very large black spider. It then flew to the ground where a number of other white doves were. It flung the spider down, and they all pecked at it and devoured it. An egg then came floating into view, and the white dove covered the egg in a nest, fluffed its feathers, and settled down to hatch the egg. The egg became the world. She was seeing a very large white dove covering the world.

"I knew then that peace was at work in the world even though at that moment the world situation seemed bleak and dark. It reassured me that this particular world problem, as big as it was, would be taken care of quickly and effectively and that, indeed, we are seeing forces at work that will eventually bring us world peace. It gives me great hope and joy."

* * *

Triggered by a vision, Carol's hope was as vast as the repercussions of war. But what about another kind of war? A war being waged by two friends against a relentless disease that threatened to take one of them away. This next story is about a woman named Margaret who found herself fighting for her best friend's life. It's about friendship—committed, unfaltering friendship. It's about a bond that is limitless with hope, boundless with love.

Margaret's friend Kim first became sick when Kim's youngest of four children was in third grade. She actually didn't feel sick until she discovered the lump on the side of her neck that was quickly diagnosed as cancer of the salivary glands. Kim and Margaret had met two years earlier shortly after Kim had obtained a divorce from an abusive alcoholic. Her life was still not entirely put back together. She was receiving only sporadic financial support and continued to be plagued by unannounced visits from her former husband, who was usually drunk, often abusive, and frequently had to be arrested to protect her and the children.

Margaret couldn't believe that the additional burden of cancer would be added to her best friend's troubles, but it was. Kim's family was unable to provide much support, so Margaret volunteered to do what she could. This amounted to child care, chauffeur service, and emotional support during the course of Kim's treatment. Margaret had no family of her own, so she had the time and energy to devote to Kim. She also had the desire to help her loving friend. It seems that both of them needed each other and loved being together. In time Kim was declared cured, and her life became more orderly. She received less harassment from her former husband, even if he didn't give her more money.

Then, less than a year later, a second cancer was found and treated. And then another. Following the third diagnosis, Margaret's own reserve of hope was too difficult to summon. Kim's kids were older and harder to manage, and she was not bouncing back in body or spirit from all the radiation, chemotherapy, and surgery she'd had. Margaret was frightened and discouraged and desperately in need of hope.

Her routine seemed fixed. "When I got off from work at 4:30, I drove to Kim's house and picked up as many of the kids as were able to go. I then drove the thirty miles to the hospital to visit. When visiting hours were over, I returned to Kim's house and dropped into bed exhausted. Then up in the morning, get the kids off to school and myself off to work, to start the routine again." By now, the kids were old enough to do the laundry, cooking, and cleaning themselves. Margaret began to wonder where it all would end; she began to doubt she would be able to survive without some respite.

Kim had only been home from the hospital about a week when tearfully she called Margaret. She felt completely discouraged, at the end of her rope, as if she couldn't go on. Her financial situation was a disaster, she didn't have the energy to be a mother, and—worst of all—she didn't care about anything any more. Margaret's throat closed from fear as she heard Kim say, "I have a large bottle of Percodan® (a powerful drug) and I think I'm going to take it." She was a twenty-minute drive away, and Margaret had never been faced with a situation like this before. And where was her hope?

In a panic, her mind went blank, but she could hear herself tell Kim to bring the pills and the phone to the bathroom. She told her to hold the receiver near the toilet so that she could hear the pills hit the water and the sound of their being flushed away. When that was done, she told her to get dressed because she would pick her up as soon as she could. Margaret then ran to her car and roared out of the driveway.

She can never remember crying so hard. "I had no idea what to do next or how to do it. I didn't know where I'd find answers or the energy to react in a useful way. I felt completely defeated. As I was speeding down the county roads, my vision nearly obscured by tears, I suddenly realized I was screaming. Screaming at God for this one last lousy trick. Screaming of pain, exhaustion, confusion, and discouragement. Screaming for help, desperate for help. I couldn't stop screaming."

As Margaret rounded the last curve before reaching Kim's house, she looked back in the direction of her small town. There, above a grain elevator, blurred by her own tears, was a perfect rainbow that appeared to end just above Kim's house. She felt as if God's great hand had been laid directly on her head. The tears and screaming stopped. Peace and hope welled up inside her again. She knew what she had to do and suddenly realized that if she would stop trying to do it all herself, divine help and energy would provide for her and Kim. Margaret had found her own supply of hope once more.

By the time she reached Kim's house, her face was dry. She was calm as she found Kim standing outdoors with a small suitcase, ready to go back to the hospital—this time to the psychiatric ward. It took only twelve hours to establish that Kim's problem was a chemical imbalance brought on by all her treatments. She wasn't "crazy" and neither was Margaret because of her revitalized hope.

Over the next three years, Kim was diagnosed with two more kinds of cancer, but medical science could only cure four of the five types she had. Margaret's hope and courage, since the day she saw the rainbow, was refueled from many sources so that she could deal with the imminent death of her best friend. Hope came from Kim's children, from dreams (hers and Kim's), from their other friends, and even from Kim's little dog, who eventually transferred its affection to Margaret.

Another source of hope came from Kim herself. "Kim and I had had many long talks in the twilight on the porch swing and we created hope in each other. And peace. On the day of her death, Kim was surrounded by her now grown children. I was at work. Everyone knew that the end was near, but we didn't realize how near. After work I drove the thirty miles once more. When I got there, Kim seemed asleep, but as I stepped up to the bed, her eyes opened, she smiled and said, 'Thanks.' Her hand closed around mine and then relaxed. She was gone."

Later, the children told Margaret that Kim had asked all day when she would be there. Margaret says, "I knew that Kim had waited for her dearest friend—for one last exchange of hope." Their shared hope had been huge enough to survive many long hospital admissions, several cancer attacks and remissions, children growing up, and finally the separation of best friends. For Margaret, her hope had been vast enough to kept her going through it all.

$$* \quad * \quad *$$

If you're in need of vast hope you must go where vast hope lives and introduce yourself. Find someone who is bigger than you are, someone with bigger ideas and broader dreams or someone who has had tougher times. It's all relative. Or go to a big mountain or a big field or a big body of water and stand there, quietly feeling the vastness around you, sensing the immense size and power that hope possesses for you. Then know that your own hope is that big and that powerful, resting inside you, just waiting to be noticed. Feel it fill you up.

15

HOPE

IS A TEACHER

*"Hope is one of
the millions of lessons
we are allowed to learn
before we return to God."*

Rick Sitz of Bradenton, Florida

ope is full of lessons for us, if we would only be willing to learn. It can be a mentor. Tapping your own inner hope for golden possibilities can be like consulting at a giant blackboard that will instruct you through your life. Like a good teacher, hope can guide you in your decisions, help you through your challenges, and remind you to do your homework. Let hope be your advisor and show you the way.

❋ ❋ ❋

A number of disturbing and unsettling events had recently occurred to Judy. The final blow came when she was fired from her job in January, just as the Christmas bills were pouring in. The next several months were depressing. She was feeling hopeless and often wondered why she had experienced such "bad luck." Then, in May of the same year, Judy met her fourth-grade teacher who told her to read Shirley MacLaine's book *Dancing in the Light.* "As I began to read that book, amazing things happened! My awareness was expanding for the first time! I somehow knew intuitively that the material I was reading spoke the truth. I viewed the world differently—like a child seeing the outdoors for the first time." She was feeling the power of her own hope.

Along with a new hope, Judy seemed to gain a new appreciation of life as, for the first time, she contemplated the concept that we are one with nature and with God. From her reading, she was coming to believe that the soul learns from each experience, and that realization gave her more hope. Her friends responded to the love she was pouring forth, and they commented on how "peaceful" Judy appeared. As her hope expanded, "My major faults, such as being critical and judgmental, had ceased—for the most part."

During this time, she also became attuned to her intuitive powers, which she identifies as her higher self. It would tell her what her body needed to eat and what action to take on certain issues. She says she was "consuming new knowledge and learning new lessons."

It had been raining a lot for a number of weeks and, as she was finishing *Dancing in the Light,* the sun broke through. "I can remember going outside and it was like seeing nature in a totally different light! It actually sparkled and the clearness was unbelievable! I even thought heaven might look like this! It was an incredible time of expansion, and for the first time in my life I felt hope. When I slip back into old beliefs, I realize that now I have learned that no matter what happens to me, positive or negative, or whoever comes into my life, I'll learn something!" For Judy, the old adage is true that when the student is ready, the teacher will appear.

* * *

Lillian was about to take a crash course in hope. From a series of painful and confusing events, she learned perhaps the toughest lesson of all: the lesson of forgiveness. Within seven months' time, her eighteen-year-old marriage ended; she was verbally accosted and physically attacked, and her new steady companion was brutally murdered. She felt victimized, alone, and frightened. Only in her early forties, she had lost faith and trust in this world and "saw this earth as a rather nasty place to be."

Because of her pain, she began to question everything she had been taught and everything she believed to be true. "I tried as honestly and as openly as I could to get to the crux of all that was. After all the debris of emotions and details had been cleared away, I began to see the essence of all that I had experienced." Like most people who sincerely look inward, Lillian found that an entirely different picture existed!

"All of my past events were showered with hurt, with feelings of abandonment, and with various degrees of fear. Thus, when I was willing to view those tragic circumstances from another level, I began to see that I had received some invaluable lessons and insights. By looking above the tragedies, I was able to incorporate the essence of forgiveness into my being and allow hope and inner peace back into my heart. I was no longer willing to allow fear and hurt to rule my life. I looked at the ugliness I perceived around me, accepted it, hugged it the best I could, and then let go of it."

The man who murdered Lillian's friend now waits in prison on death row. While she does not condone what he did, because she believed he acted on his own free will, she can now sympathize with his plight as a human being. She has come to have compassion for him. "I have chosen to remember that even a murderer is a child of God."

She says she has learned that "Hopefulness comes when we listen to our hearts and actively give expression to love. No matter how horrid the circumstances, there are always lessons to be learned and a host of good comes out of every tragedy. Whether or not we listen to the voice that offers a hopeful way to live is our own personal choice, but life goes on. So why not live with the gusto of love and hope!"

Lillian's pain and courageous inner search led her to become one of life's greatest students. Her hope was triggered by her fear and her pain, and that hope became her teacher. She has overcome some monumental tragedies and has come full circle to forgiveness and peace. She gets an A-plus.

✻ ✻ ✻

There are many ways to learn and to be taught. For a young girl named Shelley, she learned by example. During one of many surgeries to close her colostomy, Shelley, at age eleven, was pronounced clinically dead. Lying there on the operating table, she had what she calls a dream—though her description matches that of a near-death experience. First she saw light, but she thought it was the surgical lights above the table. She ignored the light and began to get off the operating table, wondering why she wasn't in the recovery room. Then she floated up toward the ceiling and over to a corner of the room.

She recalls that in her "dream" she had eyes to see but she had no form. She was greeted by an entity she could not see, but only hear. "We had a conversation that started with an offer of leaving this life and with the promise of no more pain." The entity showed her her future on the other side, but she resisted this proposal.

She was then shown her life as it would be if she agreed to stay. She told the entity that she must stay because her mom needed her. As she watched, she remembers feeling hope for the first time about her illness and about her ability to handle this life as her present self. At that moment she remembers someone calling her name. She could see through the halls and rooms of the hospital and wondered who was on the operating table and if she could help them. Shelley woke up. Her grandmother was on one side of her petting her forehead, and her mom was on the other comforting her.

As if it were on a chalkboard, Shelley learned about hope the day she viewed her whole life before her and decided to come back to this world. She brought her hope with her. She has since conquered her own health issues and gone on to teach others. "I am now a licensed massage therapist, using my own body as an example for healing." Many years ago she became her own teacher of hope and now is teaching others.

* * *

Another hopeful lesson comes from Stephen, who says, "Hope sure comes in handy in these rapidly changing times. From every direction seems to come scenes of violence, perversion, economic peril, and changes in our global environment. The fleeting vistas of hope seem ever fewer and farther in between."

Stephen considers himself a "rather observant person, readily recognizing patterns or trends, especially those that might bring about harm to myself and my loved ones." In his early twenties, he allowed the troubles of the world to concern him too deeply, even to the point of depression. Though he never really gave in to it, he searched every avenue available to him to find answers. Yet he "could find hope in nothing except for my diligence, my momentum toward finding some relief. The only thing that kept me going is that all this turmoil might end."

While Stephen was riding to work with a friend one afternoon, he began reading passages in the New Testament. It was difficult for him to concentrate on what he was reading. Rather suddenly, however, it occurred to him that he should thumb further ahead. He followed the impulse. He doesn't remember the chapter or verse or even the exact content of what he had read. He does, however, remember the message from The Book. He suddenly felt that he shouldn't overly concern himself with all the turmoil in the world, that "it would all come to terms one day; it had its purpose.

"Recounting my message makes it sound commonplace, but when it came about, I was so overwhelmed with hope that I wanted to sing." He sincerely believes "that the feelings I got from reading that day guided me to an abundance of hope." Since that time, his own hope has been rekindled by many occurrences he describes as "simple things like knowing that God was near, a brilliant sunrise, hearing a baby laugh, or simply gazing up at the night sky. More especially," he adds, "when I need hope now, the single easiest way to find hope is to give it to someone else. To help, to advise, or to simply comfort someone in need is to have all the hope you need."

His hope was awakened by reading in the Bible. Because he feels that special hope, he shares it with others. He counsels others in need of hope and gets it back. All good teachers maintain that they are constantly learning from their students. Stephen learns from the people he advises. He has had a lifetime of being concerned about the world in general, but his inner hope comes from being concerned about people, one at a time.

✳ ✳ ✳

Although Darnell is able to recall several instances when hope stirred within her, she chose one which, she considers, taught her the most about herself. She was asked to be a Sunday school teacher at her church. As was her practice, she went to her Bible for guidance and prayerfully asked her questions. Throughout the years, whenever she needed advice, she would open the Bible randomly, point her finger to a passage, and read her answer. She believes that God guides her to the appropriate passage.

Her first question was, "Lord, do you want me to be a teacher?" She closed her eyes and opened her Bible. When she looked at the page, she read: "No one begins a journey without considering the cost." She states, "By this point, I knew I wasn't prepared to be a teacher because I had no idea what the cost would be, and I was more than a little afraid." She asked a second question as she flipped to another page, "Is there anything else I should know, Lord?" Her answer came in the first phrase she read: "Perfect love casts out all fear." She accepted the job.

It was her first Sunday before a small class of ten- and eleven-year-olds of both sexes and she had little control over the students. Rather quickly it became obvious to her that one particular boy was the leader of the class. When she was able to gather the other students' attention, all it took to disrupt her rapport with them was that one boy's decision to do something other than listen to her. "He liked making spit wads best of all." Near the end of that one-hour class, Darnell burst into uncontrollable tears and explained to the students that she had never taught a class before. She wanted them to know that about her and she asked them to pray for her to become a good teacher for them.

After church, she went home very discouraged and asked God, then, to give her something that might encourage her—she would take anything. She went to her Bible, closed her eyes, then opened them to read a passage from I Kings 8:19: "Nevertheless thou shalt not build the house; but thy son that shall come forth out of thy loins, he shall build the house unto my name." At first she was confused. After all, this was no answer to her question about being a teacher. But then she considered that perhaps God wanted her to stop worrying about being a teacher by offering her hope for another part of her life. Her spirit was lifted and she instantly felt hope.

She explains why she felt so hopeful. "My family had moved to the area with the idea of building our own home, but had by then spent four years in a small trailer. We had originally hoped to build immediately, but the years had gone by without anything being accomplished. I knew then that somehow our house would be built. I went on teaching and tried to stop worrying about it." Darnell's hope for building a house was triggered by a biblical passage that didn't even relate to her current concern. Her hope responded instead to a deeper, quieter disappointment about not yet having a home of her own. Like the rest of the people in these stories, she had learned from hope. Her personal textbook, the Bible, had instructed her to work on something else and stop worrying about her worth as a teacher.

"At this writing, I'm sitting in the dining room of the house that we are still in the process of building. Everybody in the family has helped out by pounding nails, sawing lumber, and painting the walls. But the one who has worked the hardest is our son—just like the passage said. We have lived here for two-and-one-half years now. It's not totally completed, but I know it will be, eventually!

"As for the teaching, I quit about the time we started building the house. One day, during class it was as if the Lord told me, 'Darney, look around you,' and I did. I saw that I didn't have the children's attention. I knew it was time to bring in someone else with a fresh perspective. A new teacher was found for that class immediately, which only reassured me that my decision was right. Only one child expressed to me that I would be missed—the same child who made spit wads that first day of class two years before!" Darnell has learned that although she was discouraged about one area of her life, her hope was triggered for another part of her life. When she started building her house, the timing was right for her to stop teaching.

✳ ✳ ✳

Ada learned the lesson of hope many years ago but somehow forgot it. She realized that she had to go back to school for a short refresher course to relearn her old lessons in hope; they are still working today. About eighteen years ago, she found herself very desperate and down. She was in her mid-thirties, and a friend suggested that she "turn to the Father." Ada did just that and was granted what she describes as "an extraordinary sense of hope that gave me a feeling of serenity and a sense of connection to the universe. Those sensations carried me through until the late 1980s."

During that time, she was involved in a major car accident which, because of resulting nerve damage, caused her to lose the use of her left arm. She was unknowingly going through the onset of menopause, and the combined circumstances caused a major depression which, along with the drug therapies, created even more depression. Instead of turning to the Father as she had done before, this time Ada turned to street drugs to relieve both her physical and mental pain. She regained some use of her arm, but when she became a cocaine addict, she lost any hope for a healthy, happy future. She was in her late forties.

In the midst of her downward journey, Ada met a man many years her junior. He professed feelings of deep love for her. Because of those feelings and his youth, he began to follow her in the use of drugs. She had previously been arrested and was on probation for possessing cocaine but, she says, what really nudged her back onto the straight path was seeing this wonderful young person go down the wrong way with her.

"You see," Ada confesses, "I had given up. I didn't care if I died and didn't feel as though anyone else cared either. But because he did and was showing me that he did, I found the courage to tell him that I was addicted and asked him to help me stop. He did. I did. That was the end of drugs for both of us."

Sometime during the early months of being drug free, Ada was outdoors and realized that "the colors of the earth, the trees, the sky, and the houses all seemed so much more vital—so much brighter. I knew the grey veil of my former desperation and hopelessness had really lifted." Ada could feel that same hope from so long ago bubble up inside of her again. Today, she is still drug free and grateful that she was able to learn that we are always given another chance. She knows she has been forgiven.

"Some of the awful things I did or said to others during my addiction are still not healed, but I am conducting my life with the faith that healing will come. My young partner and I now own a house, and I am again practicing the art of healing others through the talent God gave me as a massage therapist." She adds, "I hated myself for becoming an addict, but God was there—not hating me but hoping I would awaken and turn to Him for help. And when I did, He gave it—full force. What a lesson I've learned! I'm constantly in awe of the love that can exist for us."

There is no limit to the number of times you can go back to school if you need to. There is no end to the number of lessons you will be given until you get it right. Hope is a patient teacher who lives inside of you and needs only to be called for a lesson, anytime, anywhere, and through any source.

✳ ✳ ✳

Lib sprained her lower back by turning over onto her stomach while sleeping. Having a history of a bad back, she had always been very conscious of not moving the wrong way. To compound matters, later that same day, she picked up a half gallon of water from the icebox and the pain went tearing, stabbing, and burning up and down her back.

She managed to get from the kitchen to her bed. The pain was agony. Even though the phone was next to the bed, she was unable to call for help because of the pain. Even if she had managed to call for help, she couldn't have gotten to the door to let anyone in.

The next day a friend called who happened to have a spare set of Lib's keys. She prayed that the phone would keep ringing long enough for her to answer. The friend came right over and stayed with her for twelve days. When her friend had to leave, she always sent another friend to stay with Lib, just in case. "I truly learned who my loyal friends were and that their friendship knows no bounds.

"The experience has left me a stronger person," she says, "and with a renewed sense in the power of prayer and my belief in God. As a result, I'm filled with more confidence and hope." She is more determined than ever to be the best person she can be in any and every endeavor, to be more compassionate and understanding and never to take anyone or anything for granted.

Lib also has more hope for her future because she realizes that before her back problem she had never really looked toward the future, but only at the moment. She was constantly living for the present and didn't completely trust tomorrow. But she is looking ahead now. Through her terrible back pain, Lib learned to trust herself, her God, her friends, and her future.

* * *

Sally is now celebrating her twenty-third wedding anniversary. There were many lessons through the years that brought her to this proud celebration. As a young mom, she was living in San Diego with her husband Bruce and their eight-year-old son Mike. Bruce was drinking heavily, and Sally was feeling increasingly frustrated and desperate. A visiting friend suggested she read *There Is a River* by Thomas Sugrue. That same day an ad on late night TV for Al-Anon prompted her to call them for information.

She read the suggested book which "immediately seemed to make everything clear. I began to believe in a higher power. I went to an Al-Anon meeting, which was a wonderful experience." She continues, "I felt relieved of my worries and learned to let go and let God. The two philosophies of Edgar Cayce and Al-Anon went together perfectly for me."

The more she learned, the more hope she had. She enrolled in a yoga teacher's training course and began teaching yoga. From that perspective, she started to focus on improving herself rather than on trying to control Bruce. An amazing change then came over him. He quit drinking. "Fifteen years later, I still read about and follow the Cayce ideas and attend Al-Anon meetings. I still teach yoga to about forty to fifty people a week, and I haven't had a cold or flu since following the Cayce diet."

* * *

Sally's hope, like all the other stories, actually came from within. Though each person encountered different reminders to be hopeful—a book, a class, a message from the Bible, or sincere caring from a friend—hope taught each of them a lesson. Their own lessons can easily be ours. Try looking for your own teaching signs. Think about what you can learn from your past sadness, pain, and confusion. Write your lesson plan for the future, and promise yourself you will reach inside for your own hope when things start getting tough. Once you've completed your lesson plan, consider doing what the people in these stories have done. Consider becoming a genuine guru of hope.

16

TOWARD A
HOPEFUL FUTURE

"... they who are weak
take hope, they who have faltered
gain new courage, they who are disappointed
and disheartened gain a new concept of hope that
springs eternally within the human breast."

Based on Edgar Cayce Reading 1436-1

The stories contained in this book offer convincing evidence that hope is available inside all of us—just waiting to be called upon. The people who have shared these stories show us how we can all experience the power of hope. They show us how, in their lives, they have learned to recognize certain symbols, sounds, and moments that triggered their supply of hope. For some, hope is awakened by a song, a cloud, a friend, a vision, a message from God, or even a book. Hope gives us strength when we need it, it gives us peace, it makes us laugh, and it keeps us humble. We see how hope can make us feel better, physically and mentally. From the stories, we also know that hope is available to everyone: young and old, male and female, accountants, drug addicts, religious leaders, and prison inmates.

As I was working with these stories, I was struck by two things. First, the stories reminded me of the many times in my own life when hope emerged to help conquer personal pain, fear, disease, or grief from the death of loved ones. Second, the stories offered me many wonderful ideas about how to tap into my own never-ending supply of hope to meet the challenges of tomorrow. By learning about how other people have experienced hope, I have learned more about my own. By understanding the many characteristics of hope, I am better able to understand how to call upon it in times of need. By reading about the many events that can stimulate hope, I now have a keener eye for recognizing the triggers of hope in my life.

Hope is indeed like a prism—a single piece of glass that transforms light into a rainbow of colors. This book offers proof that each one of us holds that prism in our hands. We have the capability, hidden deep inside us, to transform fear and pain into a rainbow of solutions because of hope. When problems touch us, it is our own individual prism of hope that can transform our pain and despair into brightly colored opportunities.

As we have learned from the A.R.E. research project participants, there are many ways to activate the powers of our hope. The first step, however, is to hold it, like a prism, up to the light. Don't let it stay hidden in your hand. Reach out with your prism of hope, be proud of your treasure, share it, talk about it, call upon it, but most important—don't be afraid to trust it to pull you through every difficult situation life may give you.

* * *

About the Author

Ruth O'Lill received her bachelor's degree in journalism/communications from St. John Fisher College in Rochester, New York.

She is a freelance writer whose work has appeared in newspapers and national and international magazines, including *Venture Inward* and *Exceptional Parent*. A former syndicated columnist, she has also written award-winning poetry as well as scripts for a comedy series which aired on public television. Currently she is collaborating with her sister on a book. Ruth lives in Virginia Beach with her husband, who is also a writer.

What Is A.R.E.?

The Association for Research and Enlightenment, Inc. (A.R.E.®), is the international headquarters for the work of Edgar Cayce (1877-1945), who is considered the best-documented psychic of the twentieth century. Founded in 1931, the A.R.E. consists of a community of people from all walks of life and spiritual traditions, who have found meaningful and life-transformative insights from the readings of Edgar Cayce.

Although A.R.E. headquarters is located in Virginia Beach, Virginia—where visitors are always welcome—the A.R.E. community is a global network of individuals who offer conferences, educational activities, and fellowship around the world. People of every age are invited to participate in programs that focus on such topics as holistic health, dreams, reincarnation, ESP, the power of the mind, meditation, and personal spirituality.

In addition to study groups and various activities, the A.R.E. offers membership benefits and services, a bimonthly magazine, a newsletter, extracts from the Cayce readings, conferences, international tours, a massage school curriculum, an impressive volunteer network, a retreat-type camp for children and adults, and A.R.E. contacts around the world. A.R.E. also maintains an affiliation with Atlantic University, which offers a master's degree program in Transpersonal Studies.

For additional information about A.R.E. activities hosted near you, please contact:

A.R.E.
67th St. and Atlantic Ave.
P.O. Box 595
Virginia Beach, VA 23451-0595
(804) 428-3588

A.R.E. Press

A.R.E. Press is a publisher and distributor of books, audiotapes, and videos that offer guidance for a more fulfilling life. Our products are based on, or are compatible with, the concepts in the psychic readings of Edgar Cayce.

We especially seek to create products which carry forward the inspirational story of individuals who have made practical application of the Cayce legacy.

For a free catalog, please write to A.R.E. Press at the address below or call toll free 1-800-723-1112. For any other information, please call 804-428-3588.

A.R.E. Press
Sixty-Eighth & Atlantic Avenue
P.O. Box 656
Virginia Beach, VA 23451-0656